BETHUMP'D WITH WORDS®

... BOOK EDITION

Covey MacGregor

❖ MLR BOOKS ❖

Warren, Vermont

Library of Congress Catalog Card Number: 98-92125
MacGregor, Covey
Bethump'd with words, book edition / Covey MacGregor
ISBN: 0-9667604-0-9
1. English language—Word Games   2. English language—Etymology
3. English language—Lexicology 4. English language—History
I. Title.

Printed and bound in the United States of America

***To Buck**
... who makes realities
out of mere possibilities*

"Zounds! I was never so *bethump'd with words* since
I first call'd my brother's father dad!" (Italics added)

William Shakespeare
King John, act II, scene 1, line 466

CONTENTS

Introduction

✧━━━━━✧━━━━━✧

✧━━━━━✧━━━━━✧

*S*peakers of English rarely profess their love of the language with the emotion or terms used by speakers of other languages. Yet love is there and it's there 'in spades.' It's an affection, however, with a revealing and peculiar difference. While the French, for example, are moved to rapture by the mellifluous sounds and poetic rhythms of their language—and, predictably, react with distain when the mood's disrupted by 'harsh' foreign entities—speakers of English love words: individual words, French words, German words, Japanese words, Yiddish words, Russian words, Melanesian words, Spanish words, indeed, *any and all* words. In sum, 'English' is less the name for a clearly defined language than for *an obsessive attitude* toward the fundamental tools of language.

This is reflected by such uniquely English phenomena as thesauri, countless publications featuring specialized compilations of words (e.g., synonyms, antonyms, homonyms, slang terms, et cetera), and a full blown industry wherein many oddly achieve success publishing nearly identical treatises: dictionaries. It is evident daily in syndicated columns, and in casual word play in every other segment of the media. There, it is salted into dialog and discussions far removed from the express topic of words. It's as though the performers and writers intuitively know their audience has a hunger that must be fed continuously, when- and wherever possible. The preoccupation is seen in the ubiquitous crossword puzzle, the unparalleled popularity of games such as Scrabble®, the never-ending introduction of word games and books of every sort. Indeed, it explains why English is now far less Anglo-Saxon than a globe-spanning melting pot of languages, the world's reservoir of *words*. It explains, too, why a lone author, the greatest word coiner, manipulator, and gamester in history, is idolized with near-religious fervor. William Shakespeare carved the mold, demonstrated models, and gave thrust and direction to an attitude toward words which has been imitated and nurtured for more than 400 years.

Bethump'd with words is an attempt to demonstrate why this is so, why Shakespeare's legacy has endured, why so many of us, his linguistic heirs, are similarly afflicted with logophilia. Instead of games that are played *with* words, it presents games that are *about* words. The focus is on the aspects of everyday words, in contrast to the obscure, that together convey the character and comprise the story of English. To a degree, it is an exposé of the factors that have contributed to English's hybrid vigor.

What U.S. coin has a name that means *goblin* in German? Ask why and you'll open a mini-capsule of history. You'll also tap into the pool of reasons that reveal why speakers of English find certain words captivating. What name for several breeds of dogs originated in the French word for *Spaniard*? In the 1990s, what professional golfer coined the portmanteau *Cablinasian* to use as an expedient way to express his racial heritage? Is the literal French meaning of *potpourri* pouring pot, little poor pot, or rotten pot? What origins are held in common by the words *shrapnel, boycott, money*, and *ammonia*? What slang term for a five-dollar bill came from the Yiddish word *finf*? What does a Melanesian mean when he says, in pidgin English, he's going to *swit mot* his mother? If you lived in the Middle Ages, why would you have taken great pains to *avoid* the joy of being *thrilled*?

When it comes to dealing with words, English—especially the American version—takes a rambunctious, fun-loving approach that says anything goes. Words are coined for any reason or purpose whatsoever. They are borrowed without hesitance from every conceivable source. They are taken apart, rearranged, expanded, combined, and in other ways massaged and squeezed until every scintilla of usefulness and, especially, comedic value is released. In the process, English sometimes does things with borrowed words that the speakers of the loaning languages never imagined, or find unthinkable or even intolerable. Howls of outrage are common features of the froth in the language's wake. But, affected by neither protest nor praise, it moves on, sublimely confident in word-handling machinations that undergird a population of unequaled creativity. The linguistic chaos and goofiness suggested by its actions do not hide the fact that English is the most powerful language on Earth.

On a daily basis, though, we tend to take our language for granted, unconsciously accepting it as an almost biological attribute like breathing and eating. English *is* a living part of us. Its mark is on every aspect of our existence, from poetry to advertising to nuclear physics to the way we think. It's a language with an extraordinary ability to express thought with precision, foster the invention of words that convey meaning with ease and accuracy, and, ultimately, accommodate societal change. Despite its tenuous start and brief encounter with the threat of extinction, today it spreads around the world with growing strength and accelerating speed. This book is devoted to the heart and sinew of our mother tongue. Its backbone is a trail that leads from primitive obscurity to global prominence. I hope you enjoy it.

Covey MacGregor

SECTION I

HIGHLIGHTS FROM THE HISTORY OF ENGLISH

A FATEFUL INVITATION

We have all heard that English embarked on its arduous climb to Global Language in the fifth century, after the 'invasion' of Britain by Germanic tribes of Angles, Saxons, and Jutes. But, according to the Venerable Bede, Britain's first historian, what became a true invasion was in fact triggered by an invitation. It was a fateful move by the Celts that proved to be an early rendition of *The Man Who Came to Dinner*.

Prior to the invitation, the Celts faced wave after wave of marauding bands of Scots and Picts. Celtic King Vortigern appealed to the Romans for help, but they had their hands full defending the Empire against similar attacks on the Continent. The world was in plunderous turmoil. In desperation, Vortigern sent an emissary across the North Sea to implore the Germanic tribes. At the time, the Saxons, Angles, and Jutes were the most powerful nations of Germany. They loved to fight, were good at it, and, he reasoned, would surely have empathy for a docile people in need.

In 449, three long ships filled with men from Jutland arrived on the shores of Britain. They and their leaders, brothers Hengist and Horsa, were welcomed with open arms by King Vortigern and his people. The foreigners immediately set to work on their assigned mission and, in short order, hammered and bloodied the barbarous marauders into a screaming northward retreat.

But rather than returning home with sated energy and a sense of noble accomplishment, Hengist and Horsa decided to look around. What they saw was mighty appealing. It is not too difficult to envision King Vortigern nervously watching the brothers' widening eyes and wondering if he had opened the Celtic version of Pandora's box.

He had. When his back was turned, the foreigners slipped home a simple message: "The land's fertile; the people are weak; we're staying; y'all come!"

And come they did, in droves that would go down in history as an invasion. To King Vortigern's consternation, Hengist and Horsa were soon leading an invincible army that, even with the passage of time, showed no signs of homesickness.

After a troubled relationship that simmered for six years, the guests turned against their hosts with cruel ferocity. The Celts, stunned and long abandoned by their Roman protectors, fought with surprising tenacity, and the battles went on for decades. Eventually outnumbered, their exhausted and dwindling population was, with finality, driven westward to the far reaches of the island.

To add galling insult to an invitation gone awry, the immigrants took to calling their former hosts *wealas*, which means *foreigners* and is the root of today's *Welsh*. By the end of that century, they also established a footing for the emergence of the language that, in its youth, was known as *Englisc*.

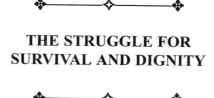

THE STRUGGLE FOR
SURVIVAL AND DIGNITY

For centuries, Young Englisc—which, for some reason, is usually labeled with reversed chronology as *Old* English—remained a primitive, crudely developed form that is barely intelligible if at all to modern users of its descendant. It had a limited vocabulary, was written in the runic alphabet, a system of mysterious origins dating from about the third century in northern Europe, and experts still get embroiled in garrulous debates about translations. Other than a few surviving inscriptions from the late fifth and early sixth centuries, the language appears to have languished in a literary slumber until Roman missionary Augustine arrived in Kent in 597. Still, Young Englisc got little real exercise. A poem here, an inscription there, another poem, and the like.

A wee bit of action came during the early years of the eighth century when the need to communicate more effectively with the pagan natives forced the Christianizing Romans to compile glossaries to ease the challenge of translating Englisc terms into their Latin. This is about as far as it went. Based on what historians have found to date, there seems to have been no interest in using Young Englisc for anything more literary. Even the Venerable Bede (c. 672-735) chose to write *An Ecclesiastical History of the English People* in mainstream Latin. It is possible, though, that more elaborate manuscripts were written but were destroyed by the Vikings, whose raids began in 778.

In any case, the historical record suggests that Young Englisc's life did not gain much in the way of dignity until sometime between the eighth and ninth centuries when an unknown poet took pen in hand and documented the story of Beowulf, a Scandinavian hero from the sixth century. The future looked more promising in the second half of the ninth century when King Alfred (849-899) came to the throne. Alfred was intelligent, literate, and determined that his people be taught how to read and write in their native language.

But just when Young Englisc's pulse began to quicken, an ominous horn-helmeted horde appeared on the horizon. Vikings. Already in control of most of central and eastern Britain, and threatening domination of the entire island, they sought to destroy the last vestige of resistence, the kingdom of Alfred. Young Englisc was terrified. The spectre of extinction hung in the balance. As Alfred faced the loathsome Danes, Young Englisc faced their language, Norse. Were the Danes to win, who knows what might happen? Would they, in vicious reprisal, destroy Young Englisc's few documented accomplishments and demand the use of

Norse by all of Britain? Could Young Englisc survive somehow, perhaps in the homes of the impoverished peasants ignored by the plunderers? The prospects of that were poor because few among the rural folk could read and write.

Alfred knew the terrible consequences of defeat as he hurriedly mustered his army and led it onto the field. The year was 878, and the place was Ethandun—today's Edington in Wiltshire. Alfred's forces formed a broad phalanx and, when the signal came, attacked the Vikings with a fury borne of terror. Swords clanged and arrows and spears whistled through the air creating a din punctuated by the grunting, shouting, and screaming of men. The bloodfest raged on until the Vikings, suddenly overwhelmed, dropped their weapons and took flight. Alfred, astonished, led his troops in pursuit. Many Vikings were caught and dispatched, while others reached the safety of a rear fortification. Alfred's men quickly surrounded it and lay in siege.

Toward the end of the second week, the weary Danes at last conceded defeat, sent out hostages, and gave their solemn oath that they would leave the kingdom. The relief was profound, and wise Alfred immediately initiated negotiations to establish a lasting peace.

Formal meetings and minor exchanges continued over the next few years, and Young Englisc, grown cocky, gleefully seized every opportunity to snatch useful and interesting words from Norse. The youth acquired what was to become the first of many handfuls. The Treaty of Wedmore, formalized in 886, reveals the language already comfortable with a repertoire of Norse that would prove durable—*fellow, landing, score, take,* and others.

In the calm that followed, King Alfred did all he could to improve the welfare of his people and to protect and enhance the acceptance and dignity of his beloved Young Englisc. Envisioning his kingdom as not only England's but Europe's center of wisdom and learning, he outlined an ambitious program of enlightenment that included translating the world's leading Latin texts into Englisc. He translated several himself, leaving unquestionable his sincerity of purpose. He implemented a momentous project when he commissioned the first issue of the *Anglo-Saxon Chronicle*.

Written in Young Englisc, it was a massive undertaking designed to bring history up to date beginning with the year 1 and the birth of Christ. It grew into a tradition that was carried on by monks in monasteries for centuries thereafter.

The extant manuscripts of the *Chronicle* are among the most important of Alfred's legacies to modern linguists. They provide an extraordinary opportunity to monitor Young Englisc's early growth and development. They also reveal much indicting evidence: the brazen youth was a hopelessly addicted word thief. It appears the young language understood even then that linguistic strength is built on a foundation of vocabulary. In time, the booty bag contained a number of Latin terms and, because many of the Danes had traded their horned helmets and swords for straw hats and plows and were easier to approach, a complement of Norse that approached 1,000 words. These included unique and easy-to-pronounce terms such as many of our *sk-* words: *ski, skin, skill, sky, skirt*, and others.

Young Englisc's position in the world of languages seemed assured as the eleventh century approached. In hand were royal endorsements, expanded acceptance, enhanced dignity, and the freedom to grow in strength and sophistication as a means of communicating. Toward the middle of that century, however, storm clouds darkened the eastern sky.

OPPORTUNITY SHATTERED?

William of Normandy sailed across the English Channel in 1066 and came ashore in Britain with an army of some 8,000 men. In a confrontation that was eerily similar to that of Ethandun 188 years earlier, Britain's King Harold faced France's William of Normandy while Young Englisc faced Norman French.

On the field at Hastings, the opponents were closely matched and the battle lasted for most of the day. But fate instantly favored the invaders when Harold and his nobles were killed. In the ensuing chaos, Young Englisc was devastated. The victory was decisive for Norman French and all appeared lost, a prosperous future shattered in a single event.

In the years that followed, Young Englisc moved ever deeper into the shadows as swarms of Norman aristocrats, abbots, bishops, merchants, artisans, and their French-speaking retinues emigrated to Britain and strengthened the foothold of their language. A spark of hope glowed briefly when William the Conqueror attempted to learn the language of his British subjects. But it died when the task, complicated by the strange runic alphabet, proved too difficult and he gave up. Young Englisc had little choice but to remain in the background, watching as Norman French, haughty in triumph, seized the role of lone favorite in the nation's halls of power. Within twenty years, the foreigner established unchallengeable control of Parliament, the courts, churches, schools, and commerce. The ultimate blow came when Britain's former upper crust scrambled for status in the developing social structure by learning and endorsing the language of their conquerors. Englisc subsequently only saw action at the top of the hierarchy when the lofty were obliged to interact with British commoners.

Between the Battle of Hastings and the early thirteenth century, Young Englisc came to realize that, in reality, it was fortunate that the Normans considered it a language of little consequence, for no steps were taken to formally outlaw or otherwise restrict its use. The neglect, though painful, was benign. Furthermore, life off stage wasn't really as awful as it seemed on that bloody day in 1066. There was ample time now to search for useful words in Latin, and even supercilious French looked ripe for the pickings. Its sounds were appealing to the ear and, comparatively, its stockpile of words was huge. When the Parisian French later sailed over the Channel to join their fellow countrymen, they expanded the opportunities by making available words from their dialect.

In the twelfth century, several ego-satisfying phenomena became evident. The French were intermarrying with the British in growing numbers, and Young Englisc often found itself in accepted and, at times, even *approved* use in social settings. Curious and more exciting was the observation that many of the aristocrats' children played with the Englisc-speaking kids of their baronial staffs and—with prescient similarity to the children of American immigrants centuries later—adopted Englisc as their mother tongue. Their affinity for Young Englisc proved so strong that they had to be taught French in school! This unexpected oddity set the young language to wondering: "Is it possible to quietly move the intruder aside and to actually reclaim lost status?"

The answer came around 1204 when seeds of distrust for the homeland were stomped into the ground by France's King Philip. With little warning, he abruptly forced King John of Britain to relinquish control of Normandy. The outcry was immediate and loud. The loss of their estates in France infuriated Britain's nobility, and their shrieking was heard from one end of the island to the other. It took 133 years, however, for their outrage to gain focus. Brandishing a compilation of France-inflicted injustices to whip their followers into a frenzy, the nobles' hatred came to a head in the outbreak of what would eventually be known as the Hundred Years War (1337-1453). British nationalism reached a feverish pitch during this period, and the fortunes of Young Englisc rose as those of French declined.

In addition to the political drama, the time encompassed a phase of the young language's life that witnessed many metabolic changes.

A TUMULTUOUS ADOLESCENCE

Scholars say the period of Middle English extended from the early twelfth century to the middle of the fifteenth. In our story, this span of time embraces Young Englisc's adolescence.

Like those of a healthy teenager, the young language's pubertal changes were physiological, complex, powerful, and numerous. The hard-to-hear inflectional endings of Anglo-Saxon were gradually discarded when, for example, it was discovered the same meanings could be conveyed by simple alterations of word order. Word order itself moved increasingly from the Germanic toward the subject-verb-object structure. While reasonable consistency in the spelling of words was maintained earlier, the language suddenly succumbed to a severe case of orthographic acne. Individual words appeared in as many as a dozen or more configurations. The Normans fomented the condition, then aggravated it when they listened to their Englisc-speaking subjects and spelled the words they heard using the conventions of French—*ceste* became *chest*, *cwen* became *queen*, *onoh* became *enough*, *huse* became *house*, and on and on. In the process, they also replaced some of the runic symbols of Englisc's alphabet with the closest sound equivalents from their Roman alphabet. This led to a major change of voice, and Englisc grew steadily less Germanic and more French-like in its pronunciations.

As a strapping youth, Englisc's appetite for words was, of course, immense. The language entered adolescence 90% Anglo-Saxon, the balance largely Norse and Latin, and left it as a 75% Anglo-Saxon by the name of *English*.

The language's raids on the larder of French climbed to a peak in the second half of the fourteenth century and eventually accounted for a period total of about 10,000 words, the substantial majority of which were nouns. Hundreds of these supplanted Young Englisc terms—for examples: *leod* was dropped for *people*; *wlitig* was dropped for *beautiful*—while others added useful degrees of difference—for examples: *house* was extended by French's *mansion*; *ox* was extended by French's *beef*.

Several thousand Latin terms from law, literature, medicine, and religion also nourished the language during the fourteenth and fifteenth centuries. This linguistic hybridizing often led to such English-French-Latin triplets as *rise-mount-ascend*, *kingly-royal-regal*, and others. Traditional usages tended to assign the triplets' English word to everyday use, the French word to literary use, and the Latin word to the snooty language of the learned.

English also added muscle to its vocabulary by coining new words and compounding and attaching affixes to others. The inclination to invent, though evident in its younger days, was now habitual and more honed in refinement. Languages encountered in the international trade carried on by the Normans, too, were natural targets, and English pilfered opportunistically from each, netting dessert-like helpings from Dutch (*skipper*), Portuguese (*marmalade*), Spanish (*cork*), Russian (*sable*), Arabic (*admiral*), and numerous others.

THE SECOND ASCENSION

English's struggle to rise above the mire of third class status—below French and Latin—and reclaim national prominence made steady progress through the fourteenth century, assisted to great extent by the mounting hatred of everything French. Around 1325, William of Nassyngton summed up the current state of affairs when he proclaimed that few, other than those who once *dwellen in cowrt* (dwelled in court), were unfamiliar with English: "*Boþe lered and lewed, olde and (y)onge, Alle vnderstonden english tonge*"—Both (the) educated and uneducated, old and young, All understand (the) English tongue.

The outbreak of war in 1337 propelled the language to the next higher tier and, in 1362, it was used to formally open a session of Parliament. By 1385, all of England's grammar schools had abandoned French for English. Fifteen years earlier, the language had discovered its most talented mentor to date when Geoffrey Chaucer (c. 1345-1400) published his *Book of the Duchess*. Other writings followed and culminated in Chaucer's most acclaimed achievement, *Canterbury Tales*, which portrayed English's use by a Medieval society that ranged from the lowly to the high and mighty.

Chaucer's work is used by linguists to mark the end of Middle English and the beginning of Modern English. For us, his work marks the end of Young Englisc's adolescent years. By then the language had grown into a robust young adult.

In the early years of the next century English met its second royal benefactor, King Henry V. To add finality to the rejection of the French, Henry knighted the young adult the official language of the land. The most significant event of all, however, occurred in 1473-74 when, on the Continent, William Caxton published the first book ever to be mechanically printed in English. In the next 150 years, the language appeared in a literary blizzard that came to an astounding 20,000 books.

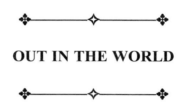

OUT IN THE WORLD

English realized it was in for a dramatically different and exciting future when the twenty-five year-old daughter of Henry VIII and Anne Boleyn came to the throne in 1558. Elizabeth (1533-1603) was a visionary and quickly proved herself the most ambitious and adventuresome sovereign in England's history. While the Spanish, Dutch, French, and Portuguese went to work to carve out positions in the New World immediately after Columbus' story got into circulation, the opportunities there were of only minor interest to Elizabeth's predecessors. For her, though, it was a chance to experience and exploit the exhilarating potential of the Renaissance.

In the midst of the excitement brought on by the Queen, English met a brilliant young poet and dramatist, William Shakespeare (1564-1616). A bond formed instantly between the two, and was stronger and more intense than any of the others in English's long history. In this fateful encounter, the language and the man became one in a manner that would survive the centuries.

Life for the language exploded with potential. With Shakespeare at the helm, adding hundreds of new words to those Elizabeth's explorers lugged back from the New World, the language of the Angles, Saxons, and Jutes stepped out of the wings and moved in confident strides to center stage.

Out in the world, English's hunger for words grew ravenous, and every language with which it brushed shoulders carried a tempting menu. Morsels and, at times, entire banquets were supplied by Amerindian, Inuit, Hindi, Arabic, Greek, Spanish, Dutch, Portuguese, the unique languages of Central and South America, the Pacific Islands, Africa, the Orient, and still others. From an island-isolated existence, the change to life in the fast lane was breathtaking.

It was also chaotic, and by the eighteenth century the need for order was desperate. New words and concepts were splattering all over the kingdom. Nearly every speaker of the language exacerbated matters with home-spun definitions and spellings. Conditions were not at all unlike the unstable metabolic period of the language's adolescence.

The concept of a dictionary had been around for several hundred years, but few authors had the language skills and, perhaps as important, the stamina to undertake a project of the size and complexity demanded by the situation. The task fell to London's Samuel Johnson. After nine laborious years, Johnson published the first significant dictionary of the English language in 1755. It was an incredible accomplishment, one that documented and, as a result of its then superior scholarship, standardized some 43,000 words. Out of bedlam came a system for dealing in an orderly and efficient way with English's aggressive word-borrowing and word-inventing propensities. The language could coin and borrow at will with the comfort of knowing there was now a place where each could be stashed and carefully tended. This first major word-reservoir also served as a model for Johnson's most prominent successors: America's Noah Webster and Oxford's James A.H. Murray.

With it, too, came world-class dignity, the most telling evidence of which appeared about fifty years later when Isaac Newton decided his classic *Opticks* would achieve wider acclaim if published in English instead of Latin, the traditional language of scientific treatises. English, puffed in pride, was no longer the ruffian youngster of the Saxons, Angles, and Jutes, nor the wild-haired comedian of the Elizabethans, it was a polished sophisticate endorsed by the world's greatest thinkers.

THE AMERICAN TOUCH

English reacted to the New World like a starved youth at a feast. New experiences, concepts, geography, animals, birds, plants, people—even strange languages—were present in exhilarating abundance. The need for new words was mind-boggling. Isolated from England by the Atlantic, the language quickly developed characteristics that brought it into closer harmony with the communication dictates of its new environment. Differences between its appearance and behavior in the New World and at home grew steadily in number and degree.

In Britain, the changes at first were ignored. It wasn't too long, however, before they began to evoke the wrath of a handful of purists, most of whom were already prone to neurotic fits over words and usages that originated outside of London. Others dismissed the changes as the products of an uncultured bunch of hooligans, as barbarous alterations in the use of the language that were, at best, inconsequential.

Colonial Americans pretended to see themselves otherwise but, in fact, were not too sure that the rough hewn images held by Britain's aristocracy were not accurate, especially when they involved the use of the language. In the colonies, linguistic insecurity existed on a massive scale. Written apologies and explanatory defenses for usages and coinings which had met challenge in Britain sailed eastward at regular intervals. Ben Franklin was among the more distinguished and subservient of the colonial apologists.

Predictably, in the 19th century, English confronted another French-like session of surgery. The colonials had won their independence and were bent on distinguishing themselves from the British in every manner possible. The imperious attitude toward their use of the language stung badly, and proved a natural target.

So inspired, Noah Webster concluded it was vital to national interests that steps be taken to *Americanize* English. The United States could, in one fell swoop, demonstrate its superiority and its repudiation of the British by pointing out their linguistic inadequacies *and* implementing improvements. Already underway was the elimination of that "wasteful" *u* in words like *colour, harbour, honour,* and *armour,* thanks in part to the conservative inclinations of Philadelphia printer Ben Franklin. It is likely the fiery Webster began by marching page by page through Samuel Johnson's dictionary. From here on out, he declared, Americans shall spell words like *tough* as *t-u-f, plough* as *p-l-o-w, group* as *g-r-o-o-p. Women* is more appropriately spelled *w-i-m-m-e-n,* and *kerb,* of course, must be spelled *c-u-r-b.* He went on.

As we know, Webster's success was only modest in this regard. But, in 1828, the success of his *American Dictionary of the English Language* was nothing short of spectacular. It charted a dramatically new course for the language. Americans now had their very own place to store invented and borrowed words. It was a depository that eliminated, entirely, the need to grovel for the approval of the British protectors of Samuel Johnson's legacy. In retrospect, the acquisition of this freedom from British domination was nearly as important as the political, for there is little doubt that America's creativity owes much to its unbridled use of the language.

Webster's audacity, of course, set off a bitter across-the-Pond debate about whose handling and nurturing of English was superior. In the early years of the twentieth century, an insult-provoked desire to prove that Americans were not second class users of the language drove H.L. Mencken to write his monumental *The American Language.* The British countered in 1928 by at last completing the scholarly work of James A.H. Murray, *The Oxford Dictionary of the English Language.* It defined nearly 415,000 words. Its date of publication—exactly one hundred years after Webster's dictionary appeared—was no mere coincidence. It symbolized a herculean yank in the superiority tug-of-war. And it was a yank that won the admiration and applause of both sides.

Today, many believe the American version of English leads the language. It is much more willing to borrow and coin than its British cousin, and its vocabulary's resulting growth, novelty, and usefulness gives the version appeal around the globe. For some, this is a worrisome condition. Troubled by American English's too-ready adoption by young consumers of *les hamburgers*, anxious guardians of French call its conquering intrusions *coca-colonialism*, to which their young cheerfully respond: *"C'est super cool!"*

Far different from the rustic language of its youth, English is in its prime of life. It is the mother tongue of 350-400,000,000 people, and is used by double that number as it is studied by millions more. Though it surely will continue to change and evolve in every conceivable way, there is no doubt about its ability to survive long into the future. In the second half of the twentieth century the Secretary General of the United Nations beamed the language out into space in the form of a message to inhabitants of the Universe. In 1969, it was spoken on the moon. In 1997, this pride of King Alfred the Great, sovereign ruler of a kingdom of illiterates, playfully named rocks on Mars.

If this abbreviated rendering leaves you hungry for more, please read on. That which remains is devoted entirely to one of the most colorful stories ever told: *the character, life, and times of the English language.*

GAME RULES

BETHUMP'D WITH WORDS®

GAME RULES

**BETHUMP'D
WITH WORDS**®

ALONE OR WITH A CROWD

You can answer the questions in the games that follow without following rules, as you sit alone with your book, pen, and pad in hand, in snug comfort by a crackling fire on a wintry evening. But, if you like the conversation that's triggered by thought-provoking issues, gather family and friends around and read the questions aloud. They're full of provocatives. And, if your crowd is typical of most speakers of English, to get through a complete game you might well have to resort to Rule One: a specified time limit on gabfesting.

The games are presented in two sections, with those in Section

I, *Bethump'd Regular*, selected and worded to provide more challenge than those in Section II, *Bethump'd Lite*. The latter feature more lingo of the young and are from the Discovery Edition of the board game. They're for your lighter moments or, especially, those times when you want to entertain the young set. It makes for an interesting travel game with backseat question readers. You'll find, too, that *Bethump'd Lite* questions bring out aspects of the language that are just as stimulating as those in *Bethump'd Regular*.

If your group includes noise-loving competitive types, it's easy to set up on-the-spot rules and a scoring system. For example, the questions in each game are arranged in progressively higher levels of difficulty (which is often a subjective determination because 'difficulty' is determined by individual experience and knowledge), so you can start by crediting correct answers for Level I questions with one point, two points for Level II questions, and so on up to six points for correct answers to Level VI questions. Competition addicts relish machiavellian twists and you can sometimes satisfy their primitive urges by suggesting havoc be wreaked with scores by subtracting points for wrong answers. You might also reward players who give correct answers with bonus opportunities or, to satisfy the deviously inclined, a say in what their opponents must do next. In any case, read through these suggestions for rules, select those that make the game fun for you and ignore the others. Or, skip over these and invent your own. In short, do whatever pleases thee and thine.

GENERAL RULES ...

✦ The question reader must read the entire question, including the name of the category. There are numerous times when the category's name is a critical part of the question.

✦ Players have the right to request a reading of the definition of a category at any time, such as before or during a game.

These are listed in alphabetical order beginning on page 27.

GAME OPTION I

Summary The score keeper determines if answers are correct *as the game proceeds*. Because the answer pages are consulted during play, this option requires one person to volunteer to read the questions and keep score. The volunteer does not participate in the competition.

1. Decide if scoring includes negative points for incorrect answers or only positive points for correct answers.

2. Decide who goes first. Players *choose* the level of question (i.e., Level I, II, III, IV, V, or VI) they want to answer. Points earned or lost are equal to the question's level (i.e., 1, 2, 3, 4, 5, or 6 points). Questions in Level I and II are easy, Levels III and IV are intermediate, and Levels V and VI are more challenging.

3. The volunteer reads the first question listed in the chosen level. The questions in each level must be used in order, that is, the volunteer cannot randomly select any question from the chosen level but, instead, must use them in the order presented.

4. After the first player answers the question, the volunteer reads the correct answer aloud and records positive points for the player's correct answer or a comparable number of negative points for an incorrect answer.

5. Play moves clockwise, and the next player chooses a question level. The game proceeds accordingly through all players, and continues to go around until all questions in the game have been answered.

6. BONUS QUESTION Players who give correct answers

to questions have the right, but no obligation, to immediately request one additional question from, and only from, the *highest* or most challenging level of the remaining questions. Correct answers to bonus questions win positive points; incorrect answers earn negative points. Play moves to the next player after the bonus question is answered.

7. **BONUS STRATEGY PLAY** If players prefer to forego a bonus question and wait until they get correct answers to each of the questions on *two consecutive* turns, they earn the right, but have no obligation, to dictate which level of question must be answered in the next turn taken by one, and only one, of their opponents. Obvious targets for this type of devilishness are the opponents with the highest running scores ... unless they're card-carrying word nerds with a talent to come up with nothing but correct answers.

8. When all questions in the game have been answered, the player with the highest score wins.

GAME OPTION II

Summary The score keeper records players' answers as the game proceeds and does not consult the answers page until all questions have been answered. This allows the score keeper to participate in the competition but eliminates the Bonus Question and Bonus Strategy Play possibilities of Option I.

1. Decide if scoring includes negative points for incorrect answers or only positive points for correct answers.

2. Select one player to read all questions or, alternatively, pass the book around as play proceeds. In this case, the opponent on the player's right reads the question from the chosen level.

3. Play proceeds as described for Option I above.

4. When all questions have been answered, the score keeper turns to the answer page, reads each correct answer aloud, then tallies scores. The player with the highest score wins the game.

OTHER POSSIBILITIES

QUESTIONS BY CHANCE If you happen to carry dice everywhere you go ...

1. Players roll one die to determine what Level of question they must answer.

2. For a fast game, players roll the pair and answer both questions.

3. For a competitive, strategy-filled game, players roll the pair, answer whichever question they want, then select an opponent who must answer the other.

THE

BETHUMP'D WITH WORDS®

QUESTION CATEGORIES & DEFINITIONS

THE

BETHUMP'D WITH WORDS®

QUESTION CATEGORIES & DEFINITIONS

The following categories were chosen because they bracket major segments of English. Together, they embrace the character of the language, the attitude and habits of its users, and cover much of its origins, history, and evolution. Although the definitions have an 'academic ring' that evokes images of desert-dry boredom, they in fact reveal the language's unique sources of strength as well as its sense of humor and many oddities. Plough or plow your way through them before you take on the games, or go straight to the games and come back only when you need them. In most instances, the wording of the question makes obvious the category's definition.

ACCENTS—*ways of speaking which can reveal places of origin and, sometimes, education and social status*. Inflection, tone, and choice of words usually characterize accents. The category often shows the range of sound and word usage English can achieve while perhaps straining but not losing communicative efficiency.

ACRONYMS—*pronounceable words that are formed from the initial letter or letters of each of a series of words, or from the major parts of compound terms.*

AMERICANISMS—*words, phrases, or expressions peculiar to American English.*

AUSTRALIANISMS—*words, phrases, or expressions peculiar to Australian English.*

BORROWED WORDS—*words adopted from other languages intact or with varying alterations in spelling, pronunciation, and, sometimes, meaning.* The category identifies English's foreign acquisitions and their original owners. It exposes the roots of the language's hybrid vigor, its word-filching practicality, its ofttimes embarrassing lack of pride of authorship, and its vacuum cleaner-like voraciousness. The category demonstrates that English's competitive strategy is to glean from others languages that which is the most useful, comical, and then some.

BRITICISMS—*words, phrases, or expression peculiar to British English.*

CALQUES—*words, phrases, or expressions formed from the direct translation of the words, phrases, or expressions of other languages.* They are an example of still another of English's grab bags, one that enriches the language with *ideas* and *concepts* invented or discovered by the speakers of other languages.

CANADIANISMS—*words, phrases, or expressions peculiar to Canadian English.*

A NOTE ABOUT Americanisms, Australianisms, Briticisms, and Canadianisms These categories focus on the dialectical nature of English. They present evidence that much of the language is based on culture and experience, but also show that the geographic isolation which led to great distinctions in the past is a fast-weakening influence in today's smaller world. They reveal, too, that each English-speaking culture reacts to the others' use of the language within a spectrum of opinions that range from 'pathetic' through 'amusing' to 'pleasing.'

DINOSAUR WORDS—*words that are archaic or are on their way to becoming so.* In some cases, these are words that are still in use but with meanings distantly removed from their original meanings. In combination with Word Origins and especially Slang, the category shows that the fringes of English are rippling continuously with life and death struggles, with weak and/or elderly words fading away as the newly coined spring boisterously to life.

EPONYMS—*words which are or are believed to be derived from the names of persons, places, or things.* The category is still another rich pool from which English draws words, in this instance with each carrying a colorful story that undergirds its accepted meaning. Eponyms illustrate that fame, infamy, humor, and, especially, the efficient or convenient filling of a definition void are key reasons why English often bestows the title of Adjective on certain names.

EUPHEMISMS—*agreeable or inoffensive words, phrases, or expressions that are substituted for those thought disagreeable or offensive for the purpose of avoiding or hiding harsh or distasteful realities.* The category underscores the language's ability to support 'subliminal politics,' those usually convoluted exploitations of its flexibility by, particularly, public figures.

GENERAL QUESTIONS—*questions that cover material outside the standard categories or which, in some way, are relevant to the story of English.* In a few cases, this category title is used because the more appropriate title makes the question's answer too obvious.

GLOBAL ENGLISH—*questions that pertain to the history, caus-*

es, impact, and status of English as a global language. The category presents evidence that the language is remarkably immune to the fevered designs and actions of those who strive to control or confine it in any way.

GRAMMAR—*the system of rules that defines the communicative structure of a language, that is, its characteristic system of inflections and syntax.* The category shows that English is characteristically claustrophobic, fights tooth and nail to shed itself of suffocating rules, and usually succeeds in thwarting the efforts of the most determined of teeth-clamped grammarians.

HISTORY—*historical highlights and milestones from the story of English.* These questions focus on the events and characters that impacted and sometimes molded English's evolution, starting with the invasion of England by the Angles, Saxons, and Jutes and moving forward to today.

HOLORIMIC PHRASES—*phrases or expressions which are heard when phrases or expressions comprised of entirely different words are spoken.* These are examples of the linguistic accidents that occur due to English's penchant for borrowing and coining like-sounding words.

HOMOGRAPHS—*two or more words which are spelled the same but differ in pronunciation, meaning, and, usually, origin.*

HOMONYMS—*two or more words which are spelled and pronounced the same but differ in meaning and, usually, origin.*

HOMOPHONES—*two or more words which are pronounced the same but differ in spelling, meaning, and, usually, origin.*

A NOTE ABOUT Homographs, Homonyms, and Homophones These categories bring out English's fondness for wise investments, that is, its inclination to borrow and coin words that offer the opportunity to 'conserve' sound and letters by leaning on the power of context. The games are designed to reflect their abundance and relative distributions in the language.

IDIOMS—*expressions whose meanings cannot be determined from the literal interpretation of the words used and/or from the combined meanings the words used.* The category reveals the breadth of the idiomatic character of English as well as its frantic drive to expand its communicative base, which it does even if it takes inventing meanings not evident in the words used.

JARGON—*the specialized, obscure, and often pretentious language of a trade, profession, or other group.* Jargon is marked by circumlocution and multi-syllable words, and is usually employed by an in-group for the purpose of protecting its vested interests from outsiders. Its earliest known definition (i.e., from the fourteenth century), which apparently was written from the perspective of outsiders, is both succinct and telling: "jargon is a confused unintelligible language."

LETTER WORDS—*combinations of letters derived from, usually, the first letter of each of a series of two or more words and which, when spoken, are expressed letter-by-letter.* For example, *FBI*, in contrast to an acronym such as *NASA*.

A NOTE ABOUT Acronyms and Letter Words These closely related categories focus on English's—especially the American version's—sometimes reckless inclination to communicate with unfettered efficiency and speed. Their excessive use has produced *Alphabetese*, a brain-numbing language spoken by the military, government, and most every other bureaucratic agency and group in the Nation. They form the fundamental units of speech in *Computerese*, wherein articles and verbs are usually the only utterances understood by outsiders. In each instance of use, however, cumbersome and/or complete and highly complex concepts are communicated with lightning speed.

LINGUISTICS—*the study of human speech including the units, nature, structure, and modification of language.*

NAMES / NICKNAMES—*names are distinctive designations of persons, places, or things; nicknames are alternate names that are usually descriptive and used instead of or in addition to proper names.* Nicknames show that English has a sense of humor that ranges from dignified and refined to weird and macabre. It makes it evident the fact that the language has an irrepressible urge to extend meanings and little patience with empty, definition-less words, like those used for names. English clearly operates with an internal by-law that says *every* utterance must carry a fair share of the load, a name *must* mean something.

PHONETICS—*the system of speech sounds of a language or group of languages; the study of the systematic classification of the sounds made in spoken utterance.*

PIDGINS & CREOLES—*Pidgins are simplified forms of speech used for communication between people who speak different languages; Creoles are advanced pidgins or languages that have evolved from pidgins and which, usually, serve as the native languages of individual speech communities.*

PORTMANTEAU WORDS—*words that are formed by blending two or more different words.* The category demonstrates that long before the bomb, English was joyfully exercising the potential of nuclear fusion, merging existing words to create others for the purpose of mushrooming its already powerful reservoir of meanings.

QUOTATIONS—*phrases, expressions, or statements relevant to the origins, history, and/or evolution of English.*

SEXIST ENGLISH—*questions related to the historical male-gender biases of English.* This category exposes a once entrenched but now teetering dark side of the language. Under attack by enlightened moderns who enjoy the slash and burn technique, English—again, especially the *American* version—is seen scurrying for gender balance via both new coinings and altered usages.

SLANG—*colloquial words or expressions derived from coinings or the arbitrary alteration of other words or expressions, and whose usual purpose is to belittle, exaggerate, or make humorous.* The category proves that many words now thought sophisticated had controversial or even low class beginnings. It shows that slang is certainly *not* a form of corruption, as purists claim, but a brimming wellspring from which many of tomorrow's most useful words might be drawn.

SYNONYMS—*two or more words that have the same or nearly the same meaning in some or all senses.*

SPOONERISMS—*phrases or sentences comprised of misplaced or transposed letters, syllables, and/or whole words.* Along with its cousin malapropisms, the category presents the comical and playful aspects of spoken English that come into being due to near-sounding word shifts, noun-verb-adjective shifts, and plain old garbled thinking. They are named in honor of the Reverend Dr. William A. Spooner, warden of New College, Oxford, a man famous for his notably absent-minded speech habits.

TRUE OR FALSE—*a question category with 50% odds.* It sometimes includes questions that overlap other categories. Like the General Questions category, it also serves as a catch-all for fill-in-the-holes-type questions important to presenting a more complete picture of the language.

WORD EVOLUTIONS—*historical and, usually, radical changes in the spellings, pronunciations, and/or meanings of words that occur over time.* The category shows what English does on those rare occasions when it finds itself in desperate need of a word to apply to a new thing or situation: it grabs an old one, shakes off the dust, and promptly crowns it with a new definition. At times this overly anxious flexibility leads to the predicament of a word with diametrically opposite meanings.

WORD ORIGINS—*a category devoted to etymology, the roots of words.* It identifies the earliest known tributaries that feed or have fed and enriched the oceanic vocabulary of English. Ultimately, the category shows that a major source of English's strength comes from its uninhibited borrowing of things useful, as well as its coining of words as needed, with each act of wordnapping and invention enhancing its ability to express thought with precision. It also makes clear the language's decided preference for words coined by comedians, in contrast to those coined by well-meaning but much too intense professional wordsmiths.

THE GAMES

SECTION II

BETHUMP'D REGULAR

Answers are found at the end of each game.

BETHUMP'D REGULAR
GAME 1

GAME 1—LEVEL I

1. **SPOONERISMS** What did William Spooner really mean to say when he blurted the phrase: "*it's kisstomary to cuss the bride*"?

2. **LETTER WORDS** Toward the end of the 20th century, what apocalyptic computer-dating problem was known in duly terrified geek-speak as *Y2K*?

3. **WORD ORIGINS** What fruit originated in China, was called a *Persian Apple* by the Greeks and Romans, was spelled *p-e-s-c-h-e* in Old French, and, when it arrived in the English-speaking world, was first spelled *p-e-c-h-e*?

4. **NAMES / NICKNAMES** In the late 1990s, what country's booming economy was known by members of the European Union's press corps as *"a leprechaun on steroids"*?

5. **BORROWED WORDS** In the 13th century, what word appeared in English as a derivative of the Old Norse word for *fear*, which is spelled *u-g-g-l-i-g-r*, and is now defined as *offensive to the sight, hideous*?

GAME 1—LEVEL II

6. **WORD ORIGINS** Sometime around 1546, what word

evolved out of the idea that *the first month of marriage is the sweetest*?

7. **PORTMANTEAU WORDS** In 1970, what portmanteau term appeared in English as a name for the dogs produced by crossing poodles with cocker spaniels?

8. **SLANG** In the depersonalized world of business of the 1990s, which of the following became known as a *cube farm*?
    a. a management staff of neanderthalic blockheads
    b. an office area crammed with cubicles
    c. a bloated yet ever-growing hierarchy of supervisors

9. **HOMOPHONES** What tribe of Native Americans is known by a French version of an Ojibwa name that is a homophone of a word that makes some in the legal profession just tingle all over?

10. **HISTORY** If *honk* appeared in English in 1835, did *beep* appear in 1529, 1729, or 1929?

GAME 1—LEVEL III

11. **IDIOMS** Astronomically speaking, what does Mom mean when she says, "*His room's like a black hole*"?
    a. his room is small and unlighted
    b. things go into his room and disappear, forever
    c. his room is like a rodent's burrow

12. **BRITICISMS** In Britain, is an *argy-bargy* an argument, a bulbous couch potato, or a party barge on the Thames?

13. **WORD ORIGINS** What substance produced from distilled wood tar has a name that originated as a blend of the Greek words for *flesh* and *preserver*, which, respectively, are spelled *k-r-e-a-s* and *s-o-t-e-r*?

14. EUPHEMISMS What word appeared in English in 1612 defined as *an exclamatory word or phrase that is obscene or profane* but did not achieve its due recognition until the 1970s when Richard Nixon produced doctored transcripts of the White House tapes during the Watergate scandal?

15. NAMES / NICKNAMES In 1913, what colloquial name was coined for *motion pictures with synchronized sound tracks*?

GAME 1—LEVEL IV

16. IDIOMS In the business world, which of the following is called a *cash cow*?
    a. a business that consumes money by the bale
    b. a business with reliably high profits and cashflow
    c. a business that, though boring, grows bullishly

17. BRITICISMS In Britain, what are the components of a meal of *bubble and squeak*?
    a. leftover beef, potatoes, and cabbage
    b. champagne and pork
    c. boiled mutton and turnips

18. WORD EVOLUTIONS In 1620, when Francis Bacon wrote the term *artillery dust* was he referring to gunpowder, outdated and rusting cannons, or the condition of buildings after an artillery attack?

19. NAMES / NICKNAMES Beginning in the 1990s, which term was increasingly *avoided* by those who name banks due to what they called "*its limiting or too restrictive definition*"?
    a. trust
    b. national
    c. bank

20. AUSTRALIANISMS In Australia, is a *drongo* a large bongo drum, stupid person, or single-lane track for kangaroo races?

GAME 1—LEVEL V

21. **NAMES / NICKNAMES** The father of American clergyman and author Cotton Mather was president of Harvard from 1685 to 1701 and had which of these as his first name?
    a. Increase
    b. Wool
    c. Extraneous

22. **WORD EVOLUTIONS** What word appeared in the 12th century defined as *obedient*, evolved to mean *full of gaiety*, and is now defined as *healthily plump*?

23. **HISTORY** What classical composition attained widespread popularity during WWII after it was realized its first four notes were the same as the Morse code for the era's most symbolic letter, the *V* of *V*ictory?
    a. Tchaikovsky's *Hungarian Dance*
    b. Chopin's *Nocturne in D-Flat*
    c. Beethoven's *Fifth Symphony*

24. **BRITICISMS** In Britain, what is a *Wimpy bar*?
    a. a fast food café
    b. a pub that sells only soft drinks
    c. a hidden, usually unlicensed, pub

25. **JARGON** In the jargon of the news media, which of these defines what is meant by *silly season*?
    a. a holiday period when employees fail to take their work seriously
    b. a period when the lack of major news stories forces the use of trivial material
    c. the time when labor contracts are up for renewal

GAME 1—LEVEL VI

26. HISTORY Since English invariably starts borrowing words as soon as it brushes shoulders with another language, in what order did these Native American words appear in English: *hogan* from the Navajo; *wigwam* from the Abenaki; *tepee* from the Dakota?

27. BRITICISMS In Britain, what is a *Scotch woodcock*?
    a. a Highlands partridge
    b. a miserly lumberjack
    c. anchovies or scrambled eggs on toast

28. EPONYMS The huge, hairy wolf spider known as the *tarantula* got its name from the city of Taranto, where it is found in abundance and which is located in which of these countries: Brazil, Italy, Zimbabwe?

29. WORD EVOLUTIONS What word started out before the 12th century defined as *a charred piece of wood*, evolved in meaning through *sword*, then *trademark*, and, finally, to *a class of goods identified by the name of a manufacturer*?

30. NAMES / NICKNAMES In 1926, which of the following brought about the use of *ack-ack* as a nickname for *antiaircraft gun*?
    a. the noise made by the gun's pumping action
    b. the coughing induced by the gun's burnt powder
    c. the British signalmen's telephone code for the letters A-A

ANSWERS

GAME 1

GAME I—Level I—1 Point Each

1. "it's customary to kiss the bride"
2. Year 2000—when, for example, it was feared that computerized accounting systems might calculate finance charges on bills as though they were due in the year 1900. Government bureaucrats were worried, too, that babies born in 2000 might instantly qualify for Medicare benefits.
3. peach
4. Ireland's
5. ugly

GAME 1—Level II—2 Points Each

6. honeymoon
7. cockapoo
8. b—an office area crammed with cubicles
9. Sioux / sue
10. 1929—the honk of a goose was imitated in written form long before the same occurred with the less natural sound of a car's horn

GAME 1—Level III—3 Points Each

11. b—things go into his room and disappear, forever
12. an argument
13. creosote
14. expletive—which appeared with stunning frequency in the

Nixon documents as "*expletive deleted*"
15. talkies

GAME 1—Level IV—4 Points Each

16. b—a business with reliably high profits and cashflow
17. a—leftover beef, potatoes, and cabbage, which are plopped into a skillet and fried together in what must be, at least in England, a noisy affair
18. gunpowder
19. c—bank
20. a stupid person

GAME 1—Level V—5 Points Each

21. a—Increase
22. buxom
23. c—Beethoven's *Fifth Symphony*
24. a—a fast food café
25. b—a period when the lack of major news stories forces the use of trivial material

GAME 1—Level VI—6 Points Each

26. wigwam (1628), tepee (1743), hogan (1871)
27. c—anchovies or scrambled eggs on toast
28. Italy
29. brand—a derivative of the word's *sword* meaning lingers on in the word *brandish*
30. c—the British signalmen's telephone code for the letters A-A

BETHUMP'D REGULAR
GAME 2

GAME 2—LEVEL I

1. **IDIOMS** Is *a mover and shaker* an itinerant preacher from New Hampshire, a rickety van loaded with household goods, or an influential person?

2. **NAMES / NICKNAMES** What name for several breeds of dogs originated in the Middle French word for *Spaniard*?

3. **AMERICANISMS** In 1775, what four-letter word appeared in English as a slang version of the five-letter word *curse*?

4. **SLANG** Does a person who knows *diddly-squat* about baseball know a lot, a modest amount, or almost nothing?

5. **WORD EVOLUTIONS** What word was once defined as *a farmer* and is akin to the Frisian word for *clumsy fellow*, which is spelled *k-l-ö-n-n-e*?

GAME 2—LEVEL II

6. **HOMONYMS** What homonyms are defined as *a hairy Tibetan ox* and a slang term for *laugh*?

7. **GLOBAL ENGLISH** In 1997, what European country's lingo cops sued Georgia Tech for using English on the Internet?

8. **BORROWED WORDS** In 1966, what Italian word was borrowed into English and defined as *a free-lance photographer who aggressively pursues celebrities for the purpose of taking candid photographs?*

9. **EUPHEMISMS** When military leaders talk about *inoperative personnel* are they referring to the dead and wounded, new recruits, or standby reserve forces?

10. **BORROWED WORDS** In 1625, what name for *a small, stand-alone shelter from which merchandise is sold* appeared in English as a derivative of the Turkish word that is phonetically spelled *k-ö-s-k?*

GAME 2—LEVEL III

11. **IDIOMS** If the IRS accused corporate management of *cooking the books*, were the company's books destroyed, falsified, or stolen?

12. **GENERAL QUESTIONS** In view of international safety standards, which of these languages was used toward the close of the 20th century by Italian pilots when they talked with Italian air controllers as they approached Italian airports in Italy: Italian, French, or English?

13. **WORD ORIGINS** In 1726, which name did Jonathan Swift coin for *a race of brutes* in his *Gulliver's Travels*: thugs, mugs, or yahoos?

14. **BRITICISMS** In Britain, are *the small stones on a beach* called pebbles, weenies, or shingles?

15. **QUOTATIONS** When the New York Yankee's Yogi Berra said, *"It's déjà vu all over again,"* was he using a palindrome, tautology, or analogy?

GAME 2—LEVEL IV

16. HISTORY Did the word *teenager* make its first appearance in English during the years 1739-41, 1839-41, or 1939-41?

17. EPONYMS In the early 1800s, Thomas Bowdler purged Shakespeare's writing of parts he thought were vulgar in order to make it fit for family reading and, as a result, contributed what word to English?

18. WORD ORIGINS The word *idiot* came from the Greek word *idiotes*, which had which of these meanings?
    a. lacking professional knowledge, a layman
    b. peculiar in behavior
    c. weak of intellect

19. BRITICISMS In Britain, if someone shouts *"Duff's up!"* does it mean your time has run out, dinner's ready, or your secret's been exposed?

20. PIDGINS & CREOLES Even though they might not speak pidgin or creole English, what *reduplicative* do most all English-speaking parents instinctively use when their toddlers reach for a hot stove?

GAME 2—LEVEL V

21. HISTORY If there were 357 publishing houses throughout the United States in 1947, by 1998 did they number about 250, 575, or 57,600?

22. BORROWED WORDS In 1579, was *china*, the generic name for the *Chinese porcelain that characterizes chinaware*, borrowed from Chinese, Portuguese, or Persian?

23. WORD EVOLUTIONS What word appeared in English in 1687 defined as *infected with measles*, evolved to *infested* *with trichinae* (nematode worms), and is now defined as *contemptibly small*?

24. **ACCENTS** What song by George and Ira Gershwin suggests that important decisions are often made based upon how a person pronounces words like *tomato* and *potato*?

25. **PHONETICS** Phonetically speaking, what is unique about the words that are spelled *c-o-u-g-h*, *d-o-u-g-h*, *p-l-o-u-g-h*, and *t-h-r-o-u-g-h*?

GAME 2—LEVEL VI

26. **NAMES / NICKNAMES** During World War II in Europe, what ethnic group among American soldiers referred to German dictator Adolf Hitler as *posah-tai-oo*, which means *crazy white man*?

27. **HISTORY** What language accomplishment is held in common by Sequoia of the Cherokee and King Sejong of Korea?
    a. each learned and spoke unaccented English
    b. each invented a written language for their people
    c. each wrote highly acclaimed English prose

28. **EPONYMS** What name for a place in Samuel Coleridge's 1798 poem *Kubla Khan* became an eponym in 1919 when it was used to mean *an idyllic, exotic, or luxurious place*?

29. **BORROWED WORDS** Use words borrowed from Japanese to complete this sentence: *If the EPA ever made outdoor barbecuing illegal because it pollutes the air, the decision makers would find it equivalent to committing political ___ over ___.*

30. **AUSTRALIANISMS** In Australia, what is a *bachelor's tart*?
    a. a feisty girl friend
    b. bread and jam
    c. an isolated or unrelated smart remark

ANSWERS
GAME 2

GAME 2—Level I—1 Point Each

1. an influential person—the expression appeared sometime around 1951
2. spaniel—from the Middle French *espaignol*
3. cuss—which was first used to refer to a person, as in "*He's a cranky old cuss.*"
4. almost nothing
5. clown

GAME 2—Level II—2 Points Each

6. yak / yak
7. France—which insisted French be used on the Web page of Tech's Lorraine, France division
8. paparazzo—the plural form, *paparazzi*, came into use as the *paparazzo* multiplied
9. the dead and wounded
10. kiosk

GAME 2—Level III—3 Points Each

11. falsified
12. English
13. yahoos
14. shingles
15. tautology—which is defined as *the needless repetition of an idea, statement, or word*

GAME 2—Level IV—4 Points Each

16. 1939-41
17. bowdlerize
18. a—lacking professional knowledge, a layman
19. dinner's ready
20. "No-No!" and-or "Hot-hot!" This reaction is interesting in that it reveals an instinctive urge to use pidgin forms when communicating with a person who speaks little or no English, including one's own toddler.

GAME 2—Level V—5 Points Each

21. about 57,600
22. Persian
23. measly
24. *"Let's Call The Whole Thing Off"*
25. each uses *-ugh* for a different sound

GAME 2—Level VI—6 Points Each

26. Native Americans, which in this case were Comanches
27. b—each invented a written language for their people
28. Xanadu
29. hara-kiri / hibachis
30. b—bread and jam

BETHUMP'D REGULAR
GAME 3

GAME 3—LEVEL I

1. **NAMES / NICKNAMES** What term appeared in English in 1935 defined as *a nitwit, kook* and was used repeatedly by TV's chauvinist Archie Bunker as disparaging name for Edith?

2. **BORROWED WORDS** If words native to English sound colloquial while those borrowed from French sound formal, which of the synonyms *begin* and *commence* was borrowed into English from French?

3. **TRUE OR FALSE** In 1844, the *goatee* was so-named because it resembles the beard of a ram.

4. **WORD ORIGINS** What name for *a person who lacks experience or competence in a sport, art, or science* evolved out of the Latin word for *lover*, which is spelled *a-m-a-t-o-r*?

5. **IDIOMS** Which fruit is associated with *jeers of disapproval*: apple, lemon, or raspberry?

GAME 3—LEVEL II

6. **WORD ORIGINS** What word that is important to academia, especially at the secondary level, appeared in English in 1622 and originated as a Greek word that means *passport* and *dou-*

bled or folded paper?

7. **PORTMANTEAU WORDS** During the 1990s, which of these portmanteau terms was coined as a generic name for the *Silicon Valley's many millionaires*?
   a. Val-moguls
   b. Silval-barons
   c. Siliconaires

8. **EPONYMS** What name of *a former official residence in Java* came into English in 1749 defined as *a miniature chicken* and later added *a person with a small stature and combative disposition*?

9. **IDIOMS** Does the term *sticker shock* refer to an unexpected fall into brambles, the reaction to a high-priced item, or a jarring jolt of electricity?

10. **HISTORY** If the printing press and the mysterious 'authority of the printed word' helped standardize *written* English, what equally momentous but much later invention helped standardize *spoken* English?

GAME 3—LEVEL III

11. **NAMES / NICKNAMES** Is *Edward Teach* better known as Blackbeard the Pirate, Attila the Hun, or John Wayne?

12. **SLANG** Which of the following comes closest to Carl Sandburg's definition of *slang*?
   a. a linguistic cesspool
   b. English's cup of hemlock
   c. English with its sleeves rolled up

13. **NAMES / NICKNAMES** During the 1990s, which slang-type name was coined for *the naive who fall prey to schemers on the Internet*: space babies, web flies, or cybersuckers?

14. WORD ORIGINS Is *cab*, as in taxi*cab*, a shortened form of cabinet, cabin, or cabriolet?

15. WORD EVOLUTIONS What word came from the Middle English word that was spelled *b-o-u-g-h-t* and means *bend*, evolved to mean *a round trip of plowing*, and is now used to mean *an athletic match, such as of boxing*?

GAME 3—LEVEL IV

16. TRUE OR FALSE The word *cleanser* came into English in the early 20th century as a trademark coined by Proctor & Gamble.

17. HISTORY If the word *race* appeared in English in 1580 defined as *a breeding stock of animals* and soon added *a people belonging to the same stock*, did the word *racism* appear in 1736, 1836, or 1936?

18. NAMES / NICKNAMES Which of the following is held in common by *Barnacle Bill, Yogi, Casper, Scooby Doo, Flat Top, Boo-Boo, the Couch*, and *Soufflé*?
    a. each played catcher for the Cincinnati Reds
    b. each is a Martian rock
    c. all were early *Boston Globe* comic strip characters

19. GRAMMAR Under what grammatical condition can these words be made to rhyme: *seek, think, bring, buy, catch, teach*?

20. LETTER WORDS What is meant by the now historic letter word *USSR*?

GAME 3—LEVEL V

21. WORD EVOLUTIONS What word started out defined as *a person who rakes manure into piles* and, around the turn of the 20th century, was used to mean *a person who aggressively seeks for publication the real or perceived misconduct of a prominent individual or business*?

22. **WORD ORIGINS** In the late 16th century, was *braggadocio*, which means *braggart*, coined by a French, Italian, or English poet?

23. **GLOBAL ENGLISH** In 1933, what author of *The Shape of Things to Come* imagined, as he wrote, *"a world free from conflict in which English would be an international medium capable of expressing previously inaccessible ideas"*?
    a. Raymond Bradbury
    b. Herbert George Wells
    c. George Orwell

24. **BRITICISMS** In Britain, is a *clinker* something that is first rate, a flop, or a fist-size rock?

25. **BORROWED WORDS** In 1806, English borrowed the Shawnee Indian word *wapiti* as the name for an animal even though it already had what perfectly adequate synonym?

GAME 3—LEVEL VI

26. **WORD EVOLUTIONS** In Elizabethan England was *a man's cap* known as a bonnet, toque, or beanie?

27. **LETTER WORDS** What is meant by the *ISV* that follows dictionary listings of words like *saccharin* and *glyceric acid*?

28. **BORROWED WORDS** In 1837, was the term *hoi polloi*, which means *the masses*, borrowed from Latin, Greek, or Yiddish?

29. **NAMES / NICKNAMES** Was *siren*, *echo*, or *vapor* the name of the nymph in Greek mythology who fell in love with

Narcissus and pined away until nothing was left of her but her voice?

30. WORD EVOLUTIONS In the 16th century, what word was defined as *to pierce with a sword* and now means *to experience a sudden sharp feeling of excitement*?

ANSWERS

GAME 3

GAME 3—Level I—1 Point Each

1. ding-a-ling
2. commence
3. False—it was so-named because it resembles the beard of a buck, a male *goat*. A *ram* is a male sheep.
4. amateur
5. raspberry—as in "The fans gave Casey the *raspberries* when he struck out."

GAME 3—Level II—2 Points Each

6. diploma
7. c—Siliconaires, a blend of *Silicon + millionaires*
8. bantam
9. the reaction to a high-priced item
10. radio

GAME 3—Level III—3 Points Each

11. Blackbeard the Pirate
12. c—English with its sleeves rolled up
13. cybersuckers
14. cabriolet—which is a one-horse carriage that was called a *cab* as early as 1827
15. bout

GAME 3—Level IV—4 Points Each

16. False—it appeared in English before the 12th century
17. 1936
18. b—each is a rock encountered on Mars by little rover Sojourner that was named by the NASA JPL team in July 1997
19. use each in the past tense
20. *U*nion of *S*oviet *S*ocialist *R*epublics

GAME 3—Level V—5 Points Each

21. muckraker
22. English—it came from *Braggadoccio*, a character who is the personification of boasting in Edmund Spenser's *Faerie Queene*
23. b—Herbert George Wells
24. something that is first rate
25. elk—in Shawnee, *wapiti* has the literal meaning of *white rump*

GAME 3—Level VI—6 Points Each

26. bonnet—*toques* were worn by women and *beanie* didn't appear in English until 1940
27. it indicates the word is part of the *I*nternational *S*cientific *V*ocabulary
28. Greek
29. echo
30. thrill

BETHUMP'D REGULAR
GAME 4

GAME 4—LEVEL I

1. **EPONYMS** What slang term for *handgun* appeared in English in 1904 as a derivative of the name of American inventor Richard J. Gatling?

2. **GRAMMAR** What will you be advised to avoid if a dedicated grammarian hears you say, *"I don't never want to go'"*?

3. **SEXIST ENGLISH** In English's historical gender-biased usages, what was usually the gender of the person who was described as *the strong silent type, a person of few words*?

4. **WORD ORIGINS** What country's name came from the Latin term *Terra Australis*, which means *the southern land*?

5. **IDIOMS** Idiomatically speaking, is a person who was the victim of *a snow job* one who was clobbered with a snowball, one who was forced to take a ski instructor's position, or one who was deceived or persuaded by intensive means?

GAME 4—LEVEL II

6. **SLANG** In 1970, which of these terms was coined and defined as *something that tastes disgusting*: yucky, ugsome, or roadkill?

7. **BORROWED WORDS** What word did English derive from the Dutch word that is spelled *d-e-k-k-e-n* and is used to mean *to clothe elegantly* and, in slang, *to knock down*?

8. **TRUE OR FALSE** In contrast to the lax habits of the time, William Shakespeare helped establish an attitude favoring consistency in the spelling of personal names by maintaining rigid consistency in the spelling of his own.

9. **GENERAL QUESTIONS** What American sport is known in Japlish, the Japanese-English hybrid language, by a word that is phonetically spelled *b-e-s-u-b-o-r-u*?

10. **LETTER WORDS** What U.S. government agency oversees and regulates the shipment of goods from state to state and is known as the *ICC*?

GAME 4—LEVEL III

11. **NAMES / NICKNAMES** Which of the following explains why, in 1896, Wilhelm Röentgen named the rays he discovered *X-rays*?
    - a. it was his tenth major discovery
    - b. he loved the music of *X*avier Cugat
    - c. he was clueless when it came to understanding the nature of the rays

12. **BORROWED WORDS** The word *boudoir* means *a woman's dressing room or bedroom* and originated in the French word *bouder*, which has which of these meanings?
    - a. to powder
    - b. to pout
    - c. to bow out

13. **BRITICISMS** Does the British euphemistic statement *"He's assisting the police"* mean he's a stool pigeon, an overzealous do-gooder, or a criminal suspect?

14. AUSTRALIANISMS In Australia, is a *joey* a baby animal, small cup of coffee, or joyous occasion?

15. WORD EVOLUTIONS Which of the following gave rise to the term *stool pigeon*?
> a. the hunters' practice of tying decoy birds to stools
> b. the use of stools in church confessionals
> c. the repulsive sanitary habits of pigeons

GAME 4—LEVEL IV

16. ACCENTS During the televised opening ceremonies of the 26th Olympiad, IBM featured English-speaking Australians in commercials that were enhanced for U.S. listeners by which of these techniques?
> a. a two-fold increase in sound volume
> b. the use of subtitles
> c. a slowed sound track

17. HOMOPHONES If a careless cook serves scorched chopped leaves and stalks from Swiss beets, the dish could be called ___ ___.

18. EPONYMS Which was first to roll out of Conestoga, Pennsylvania, the cigar known as a *stogie* or the wagon known as the *Conestoga*?

19. SLANG Which definition of the word *cop* was first to appear in English: *to steal* or *police officer*?

20. BRITICISMS In Britain, which of these names is used for *a container that is placed on the table for receiving the dregs of tea and coffee*?
> a. slop bowl or slop basin
> b. Tee-cee hopper
> c. grounds keeper

GAME 4—LEVEL V

21. HISTORY If the world now has about 6,000 languages, how many do some language experts predict will exist by the end of the 21st century?
    a. 7,500, an increase of 25%
    b. 6,006, an almost negligible increase
    c. 600, a loss of 90%

22. IDIOMS What ruminant-based term appeared in English in 1910 defined as *a thing that is unreasonably immune from criticism or opposition*?

23. WORD ORIGINS In 1982, which of these words did William Gibson coin and publish in his short story *Burning Chrome*, then popularize in his 1984 best seller *Neuromancer*?
    a. Internet
    b. cyberspace
    c. World Wide Web

24. LETTER WORDS What is the meaning of the Latin term *exempli gratia*?

25. BORROWED WORDS Identify and spell the word that is a combination of the German words for *wonder* and *child* and was borrowed into English in 1891 defined as *a child prodigy*.

GAME 4—LEVEL VI

26. SLANG What slang-type term defined as *to bargain* and *to haggle over price* evolved out of the Latin word that is spelled *d-e-c-u-r-i-a* and means *a set of ten*?

27. WORD EVOLUTIONS Which of the following is the modern translation of the Anglo-Saxon's nickname for the fearsome Vikings, which is spelled *w-a-e-l-w-u-l-f-a-s*?
    a. whale gulpers

b. wall breakers

c. slaughterous wolves

28. BORROWED WORDS What expression is thought to have evolved from the English pronunciation of the Dutch words that mean *a lost band*, such as might occur with *a band of men selected for an extremely hazardous military mission*, and are spelled *v-e-r-l-o-r-e-n h-o-o-p*?

29. GLOBAL ENGLISH In Germany, which of these American TV programs was the only listed with its name germanicized in the March 11, 1995 edition of the *Frankfurter Allgemeine Zeitung*?

a. *The A-Team*

b. *Beverly Hills 90210*

c. *Melrose Place*

30. BRITICISMS In a dialect of Northern England, what is meant if someone uses a word that is phonetically spelled *o-w-t* in a sentence like: *"Can I get you owt"*?

a. What do I have to do to get you to leave?

b. Can I get you anything? (such as a drink)

c. Can I get you to be quiet while I talk?

ANSWERS

GAME 4

GAME 4—Level I—1 Point Each

1. gat—a shortened form of *Gatling Gun*, which is the machine gun Gatling invented in the 1860s
2. double negatives
3. male
4. Australia's
5. one who is deceived or persuaded by intensive means

GAME 4—Level II—2 Points Each

6. yucky
7. deck—which appeared in English in 1513
8. False—Shakespeare, too, did not feel compelled to write his own name with consistency and wrote it with several different spellings
9. baseball
10. *I*nterstate *C*ommerce *C*ommission

GAME 4—Level III—3 Points Each

11. c—he was clueless when it came to understanding the nature of the rays
12. b—to pout
13. a criminal suspect
14. baby animal—especially a baby kangaroo
15. a—the hunters' practice of tying decoy birds to stools

GAME 4—Level IV—4 Points Each

16. b—the use of subtitles, which is usually done when someone is speaking a foreign language
17. charred / chard
18. wagon (1717) / cigar (1853)
19. to steal (1704) / police officer (1859)
20. a—slop bowl or slop basin

GAME 4—Level V—5 Points Each

21. c—600, a loss of 90%
22. sacred cow—which came from the veneration of the cow by the Hindus
23. b—cyberspace
24. for example—which is usually written in the abbreviated form *e.g.*
25. *w-u-n-d-e-r-k-i-n-d*

GAME 4—Level VI—6 Points Each

26. dicker
27. c—slaughterous wolves
28. forlorn hope
29. a—*The A-Team*, which was listed as *Das A-Team*
30. b—Can I get you anything? (such as a drink)

BETHUMP'D REGULAR
GAME 5

GAME 5—LEVEL I

1. **SLANG** What altered form of the word *divide* appeared in English in 1877, is defined as *to share*, and is usually used in combination with the word *up*?

2. **EPONYMS** In 1878, a variety of which fruit was named after 18th century Canadian settler John McIntosh: peach, apple, or pear?

3. **WORD ORIGINS** In 1670, what word came into English as a derivative of the Latin word that is spelled *j-o-c-u-s* and defined as *something said or done to provoke laughter*?

4. **NAMES / NICKNAMES** What nickname was born on August 19, 1812 when cannonballs fired by the British frigate *H.M.S. Guerrière* bounced feebly off the thick wooden side of the *U.S.S. Constitution*?

5. **HOMONYMS** What homonyms are found on calendars and tall palms with pinnate leaves?

GAME 5— LEVEL II

6. **HOMOPHONES** Identify and spell the homophones defined as:
    a. a slide or sloping channel through which things are

passed downward
b. to drive forth by an explosion

7. **WORD ORIGINS** What is the meaning of the Latin term *id est*, which is usually used in the abbreviated form *i.e.*?

8. **EPONYMS** The name of an old German coin is spelled *t-a-l-e-r,* short for Joachims*taler* which means *of or from Joachimsthal*, a town in Bohemia where the coin was made. The name was spelled *d-a-l-e-r* in Low German which, in 1553, was borrowed into English and anglicized into what word?

9. **HISTORY** What word game found in many daily newspapers was invented by Arthur Wynne and made its first appearance on December 21, 1913 in the *New York World*?

10. **WORD EVOLUTIONS** During the politically turbulent years of the Vietnam War, what birds' names acquired new meanings when they were used to categorize the war's *proponents* and *opponents*?

GAME 5—LEVEL III

11. **SLANG** In 1977, which term was coined for *a place where stolen automobiles are stripped of saleable parts*: strip joint, pit stop, or chop shop?

12. **WORD ORIGINS** The word that is spelled *p-a-n-t* appeared in English in 1840 defined as *an outer garment covering each leg separately, usually extending from the waist to the ankle* and is a shortened form of what word?

13. **AMERICANISMS** In 1929, what borough of New York City gave its name to *a raspberry cheer*?

14. **WORD ORIGINS** During the 13th century, what word

evolved out of the Latin term *comes stabuli*, which literally means *officer of the stables*?

15. **SLANG**   In military slang, is *a soldier in full dress, including helmet, flak jacket, and automatic weapon*, said to be wearing battle rattle, play clothes, or Mommy's comforts?

GAME 5—LEVEL IV

16. **HOMOGRAPHS**   Identify and spell the homographs defined as:
    a. a fluid dressing that adds zest to food
    b. impudent language, back-talk

17. **HOMOPHONES**   Identify and spell the homophones defined as:
    a. an Italian greeting
    b. a slang term for *food* that was borrowed from Chinese Pidgin English

18. **PORTMANTEAU WORDS**   What long-tailed raptor has a name that came from a blend of the Old English words for *goose* and *hawk*?

19. **WORD ORIGINS**   What common name for a particular year in secondary or undergraduate school is thought to be derived from a combination of the Greek words for *wise* and *foolish*?

20. **WORD EVOLUTIONS**   In the early 17th century, which of these words was defined as *unnatural, adulterated, impure*, and now is used largely to mean *refined in experience and awareness*?
    a. sophisticated
    b. polished
    c. debonair

GAME 5—LEVEL V

21. WORD ORIGINS During the 13th century, the Old English word that is spelled *e-a-g-t-h-y-r-e-l* and means *eye-hole* was gradually displaced by the Old Norse word that is spelled *v-i-n-d-a-u-g-a*, which means *wind's eye* and is the ancestral root of what modern word?

22. NAMES / NICKNAMES Which of the following is the source of the *Jove* that is used in expressions like: "*By Jove, she was voted in as president*"?
    a. Joseph Velaccio
    b. the planet Jupiter
    c. Joseph, husband of Jesus' mother, Mary

23. JARGON In 1975, what name was coined for the *computer parameter that comprises 1,073,741,824 bytes*?

24. IDIOMS To what period of life was Shakespeare referring when he wrote the phrase *"my salad days"*?
    a. the time of youthful inexperience and indiscretion
    b. the prime of life
    c. the wilting years of old age

25. BORROWED WORDS Experts claim that when two languages show no trace of exchanged or borrowed words, it is safe to say which of the following:
    a. enmity exists between the speakers of each
    b. they have had no contact with each other
    c. neither has an educated population

GAME 5—LEVEL VI

26. SLANG What slang term appeared in English in 1700 defined as *in an irresolute or indecisive manner* and, in linguistics terms, is called an 'irregular reduplicative' of the phrase *shall I*?

27. PORTMANTEAU WORDS In the jargon of language rights advocates, what portmanteau word was coined during the early 1990s and defined as *linguistic racism*?

28. WORD ORIGINS What word came from the Latin word for *red*, which is spelled *r-u-b-e-r*, was used in Middle English to mean *a heading in red letters*, and is now defined as *an authoritative rule*?

29. NAMES / NICKNAMES Before Japanese women began to openly object to male chauvinism, were the *women who were unmarried by age twenty-five* called the Japanese equivalent of leftovers, Christmas cakes, or stale cookies?

30. HISTORY In 1755, which letter of our alphabet did Samuel Johnson define as *"... a letter of which the form is not to be found in the alphabets of (any of) the learned languages"*?

ANSWERS

GAME 5

GAME 5—Level I—1 Point Each

1. divvy
2. apple
3. joke
4. Old Ironsides
5. dates / dates

GAME 5—Level II—2 Points Each

6. *c-h-u-t-e* / *s-h-o-o-t*
7. that is
8. dollar
9. crossword puzzle—which initially was called a *word cross*
10. hawks (proponents) / doves (opponents)

GAME 5—Level III—3 Points Each

11. chop shop
12. pantaloons
13. The Bronx—as in *"When the Babe stuck out, the raucous crowd gave him a Bronx cheer."*
14. constable
15. battle rattle

GAME 5—Level IV—4 Points Each

16. *s-a-u-c-e* / *s-a-u-c-e*
17. *c-i-a-o* / *c-h-o-w*
18. goshawk
19. sophomore—which appeared in 1688, most likely from the combination of the Greek words *sophos* (wise) + *moros* (foolish). *Moros* is perhaps better known as the root of *moron*.
20. a—sophisticated

GAME 5—Level V—5 Points Each

21. window
22. b—the planet Jupiter. The term evolved out of the Latin prefix for planet's name, *Jov-*
23. gigabyte
24. a—the time of youthful inexperience and indiscretion
25. b—they have had no contact with each other

GAME 5—Level VI—6 Points Each

26. shilly-shally
27. linguicism—which appeared in Robert Phillipson's *Linguistic Imperialism* (1992) and which some say is really a portmanteau of *linguistically 'argued' racism*
28. rubric
29. Christmas cakes
30. w

BETHUMP'D REGULAR
GAME 6

GAME 6—LEVEL I

1. **LETTER WORDS** What group of fluoride pushers is known as the *ADA*?

2. **EPONYMS** What state within the United States was named after a virgin queen?

3. **TRUE OR FALSE** As it is in mathematics, in English the use of double negatives in a sentence reverses meaning and communicates a positive.

4. **SEXIST ENGLISH** In English's historical stereotyping of gender-linked speech, which gender was considered more likely to use the words *adorable* and *lovely*?

5. **NAMES / NICKNAMES** Toward the end of WWII, what name was coined for *the letter in which a man, usually a soldier, was informed that his girlfriend, fiancée, or spouse wanted to sever their relationship*?

GAME 6— LEVEL II

6. **JARGON** Which of these U.S. industries gave English the idiom *make the grade*?
   a. railroad
   b. steel

c. automotive

7. **PORTMANTEAU WORDS** Toward the end of the 20th century, what two languages began to hybridize to form a language now known as *Russlish*?

8. **EPONYMS** In addition to their social status, which meat is held in common by the *Duke of Wellington* and *Count Paul Stroganoff*: pork, beef, or mutton?

9. **LETTER WORDS** What is meant if a formal invitation to a party includes, at the bottom, the letter word *BYOB*?

10. **HOMOGRAPHS** Identify the homographs in this sentence: *The Company's officers signed a ___ that claimed the steel manufactured by the Company would not ___ more than 0.1% in prolonged sub-zero weather.*

GAME 6—LEVEL III

11. **BRITICISMS** What do the British call the *pull tab on a can*?
    a. a tin ear
    b. a manhole cover
    c. an automatic can opener

12. **HOMOPHONES** Identify and spell the homophones defined as:
    a. a prominent, well-defined summit
    b. a transient feeling of wounded vanity

13. **WORD EVOLUTIONS** What word appeared in 1818 defined as *a horse for riding or driving on roads*, then evolved in the early 20th century to include the automobile described as *a two-seat convertible with a rear luggage compartment*?

14. BORROWED WORDS What word appeared in English in the 13th century as an anglicized version of the French word that is spelled *b-o-u-t-e-i-l-l-i-e-r* and means *bottle carrier*?

15. IDIOMS In 1909, what hoggish name was coined for *government projects involving large amounts of taxpayers' money that politicians shunt to their friends*?

GAME 6—LEVEL IV

16. BORROWED WORDS Which of these borrowed words eventually displaced the Old English word that is spelled *t-w-i-e-w-i-f-i-n-g*?
   a. zwieback, from German
   b. bigamy, from Latin
   c. twining, from Norse

17. GENERAL QUESTIONS What characteristic is held in common by Shakespeare's *Mrs. Quickly*, Fielding's *Mrs. Slipslop*, Sheriden's *Mrs. Malaprop*, and Shillaber's *Mrs. Partington*?
   a. a burning desire to use large words
   b. a comical avoidance of large words
   c. a tendency to misapply or distort large words

18. WORD ORIGINS What slang-type word is defined as *a friend of long standing* and evolved out of the Greek word that means *long lasting* and is spelled *c-h-r-o-n-i-o-s*?

19. HOMONYMS What single, slang-type word is often used with such diverse meanings as *bag, bed, dismissal, plunder, tackle,* and *white wine*?

20. PORTMANTEAU WORDS In 1897, what word was coined as a blend of *happen* and *circumstance* and defined as *a circumstance due to chance*?

GAME 6—LEVEL V

21. **HISTORY** Which of the following explains why the Anglo-Saxons were using a word equivalent to *church* long before their conversion to Christianity?
    a. they were superstitious and feared the Christian God
    b. their ancestors plundered Rome's churches
    c. they worshiped Woden and Thor in a similar building

22. **IDIOMS** In what order did the terms *hog wild*, *hog heaven*, and *hogwash* appear in English?

23. **HOMONYMS** What homonyms came from a 14th century word defined as *a brownish dark gray color* and a 17th century word that is an eponym defined as *to make persistent demands for payment*?

24. **AMERICANISMS** Because Germans typically spend their working lives with one company, the German language lacked a precise, uncompounded name for *a part-time position* until it borrowed what word during its exposure to American English and the more 'employment-mobile' attitude of Americans?

25. **IDIOMS** Which of these is the source of the idiom *feet of clay*, which is defined as *a character flaw that is not readily apparent*?
    a. Chaucer's *Canterbury Tales*
    b. Shakespeare's *Hamlet*
    c. the Bible's *Book of Daniel*

GAME 6—LEVEL VI

26. **SEXIST ENGLISH** If, in the 14th century, *patrimony* was defined as *an estate inherited from one's father or ancestor*, what was the 14th century definition of *matrimony*?
    a. an estate inherited from one's mother or one of her ancestors

b. an estate inherited from one's aunt

c. marriage

27. AMERICANISMS What French expression that was borrowed and used in English ever since 1845 got colloquial competition in 1979 when Americans started using the expression *done deal*, such as in *"It's a done deal"*?

28. BORROWED WORDS Which of the following is the original meaning of the Hindi root of *seersucker*, which is defined in English as *a light, usually striped and puckered linen, cotton, or rayon fabric*?

a. fortune teller's fool

b. milk and sugar

c. kissing lips

29. HOMONYMS Identify the homonyms that have roots in the following:

a. the Old English word for *spot*

b. the Middle Dutch word for *earth thrower*

c. the German word that is short for *molecular weight*

30. LINGUISTICS What do linguists call *words that are coined expressly for one occasion or use*, such as *Excaliburgers*, the name given to hamburgers sold at a site associated with legendary King Arthur in Cornwall, England?

a. nonce words

b. nosh words

c. singlets

ANSWERS

GAME 6

GAME 6—Level I—1 Point Each

1. *A*merican *D*ental *A*ssociation
2. Virginia—in honor of Queen Elizabeth I, who was known as "the Virgin Queen"
3. False—there is usually no misunderstanding the sad and profound negativity in a sentence like *"I don't got no money"*
4. female
5. Dear John

GAME 6—Level II—2 Points Each

6. a—railroad
7. *Russ*ian + Eng*lish*
8. beef
9. *B*ring *Y*our *O*wn *B*ottle (or *B*ooze or *B*eer or *B*everage)
10. contract / contract

GAME 6—Level III—3 Points Each

11. c—an automatic can opener
12. *p-e-a-k* / *p-i-q-u-e*
13. roadster
14. butler
15. pork barrel

GAME 6—Level IV—4 Points Each

16. b—bigamy, from Latin
17. c—a tendency to misapply or distort large words
18. crony
19. sack
20. happenstance

GAME 6—Level V—5 Points Each

21. b—their ancestors plundered Rome's churches and, thus, they were quite familiar with the word
22. hogwash (15th century), hog wild (1904), hog heaven (1945)
23. dun / dun
24. job—which, as *Der Job*, is now a German term defined as *temporary employment*
25. c—the Bible's *Book of Daniel*, 2:33

GAME 6—Level VI—6 Points Each

26. c—marriage, which makes the combination unlike the more consistent relationship that exists between the meanings of *patriarchy* and *matriarchy*
27. *fait accompli*
28. b—milk and sugar
29. mole
30. a—nonce words

BETHUMP'D REGULAR
GAME 7

GAME 7—LEVEL I

1. **EPONYMS** What word came from the Greek word that is spelled *t-i-t-a-n-i-k-o-s*, which means *of the Titans*, is now defined as *having great size, power, or force*, and was once used as the name of a doomed ship?

2. **SLANG** Which of the following appeared in 1605 as a disparaging term for *a person who lacks courage*?
    a. lily-livered
    b. fruitcake
    c. bum

3. **IDIOMS** What animal is terribly abused in idioms that feed it a cast of pearls, put it in a poke, and use part of its anatomy to make a silk purse?

4. **HOLORIMIC PHRASES** What word did the chemist think of when the telephone company called to say it was giving all customers special *night rates*?

5. **BORROWED WORDS** In 1599, what name for a type of hat appeared in English as a derivative of the Spanish word that is spelled *s-o-m-b-r-a* and means *shade*?

GAME 7—LEVEL II

6. **TRUE OR FALSE** The *Dutch* in the name *Pennsylvania Dutch* evolved out of the local mispronunciation of the German word that is spelled *D-e-u-t-s-c-h* and means *German*.

7. **ACCENTS** The aitch-less speech of London's Cockneys makes the word *heady* a homophone of what word that is defined as *a contrary current?*

8. **BORROWED WORDS** Which of the following synonyms for *to depart quickly* was derived from Spanish in 1840?
   a. scram
   b. skedaddle
   c. vamoose

9. **LETTER WORDS** What regulator of Wall Street's favorite activity is known as the *SEC?*

10. **IDIOMS** What fruity, idiomatic term is usually used to classify the complaints of the person who is consumed with bitterness?

GAME 7—LEVEL III

11. **SLANG** In 1997, which name was coined by inline skaters for *the burns and scrapes suffered as a result of not wearing protective gear?*
    a. scrapurns
    b. road rash
    c. skate steak

12. **HOMOGRAPHS** Identify the homographs defined as:
    a. to strike sharply, especially with the hand
    b. a meal set out on a table for ready access and informal service

13. GLOBAL ENGLISH A worldwide survey showed that by mid-1997 English was the language of 82.3% of the Net's home pages. What two languages were next in line with 4% and 1.6% respectively?
   a. French & Spanish
   b. Italian & Russian
   c. German & Japanese

14. BORROWED WORDS In 1826, what French term that has the literal meaning of *by the bill of fare* was borrowed intact into English for use, primarily, in the jargon of restaurants?

15. DINOSAUR WORDS What is meant by the *quick* in the phrase *the quick and the dead*?
   a. the living
   b. the fast
   c. the intelligent

GAME 7—LEVEL IV

16. BORROWED WORDS While English used *naught* to cover the concept of *nothing* before the 12th century, it lacked a term for the mathematical concept of *the absence of all quantity* until about 1604 when it borrowed from French what word that originated in Arabic?

17. SLANG At the turn of the 20th century, which of these words was labeled in Britain as *"a cheap and vulgar product of trans-Atlantic—i.e., American—slang"*?
   a. bawdy
   b. obscene
   c. scientist

18. CALQUES In the late 20th century, what English term was borrowed into German where it is spelled *f-r-i-e-d-l-i-c-h-e K-o-e-x-i-s-t-e-n-z*?

19. AUSTRALIANISMS In Australia, is a *milko* a milkman, dairy cow, or the drink known to Americans as a White Russian?

20. EPONYMS In 1958, what facetious legal term came into English with the name of American engineer Edward A. Murphy?

GAME 7—LEVEL V

21. WORD EVOLUTIONS Which appeared first in English, *gnarl*, which means *to deform by twisting*, or *gnarled*, which means *full of knots*?

22. GLOBAL ENGLISH Which of the following sums up the findings of a 1990s survey of jobs described in help wanted ads in Poland's newspapers?
  a. 46% required knowledge of English
  b. 46% said the use English was not tolerated by their company or organization
  c. 46% oddly said fluency in Polish was essential

23. SEXIST ENGLISH What did CBS network officials conclude about the voice of broadcast journalist Betty Watson after she reported the Nazi invasion of Norway on April 12,1940?
  a. it is too young and feminine for war news
  b. compared with the voices of male news journalists, its higher pitch creates an aura of urgency
  c. its femininity and uniqueness will attract advertisers

24. ACCENTS In the early years of its existence, was it Britain's BBC or America's NBC which insisted that its radio announcers have *"clear enunciation and a pronunciation free of dialect and local peculiarities"*?

25. WORD EVOLUTIONS What word was once defined as

fate or destiny, was used by Shakespeare when he wrote about the three Norse goddesses of fate, the Norns, and is now used to mean *odd, unearthly, mysterious*?

GAME 7—LEVEL VI

26. **BRITICISMS** In Britain, what does a person from Yorkshire intend to do when he says, *"I'm going to addle some brass"*?
    a. make some money
    b. upset some bigwigs
    c. participate in the British equivalent of a demolition derby

27. **BORROWED WORDS** What Italian term has the literal meaning of *Frankish* (French) *language* but is used in English to mean *resembling a common language, such as that spoken between people of diverse speech*?

28. **EPONYMS** What slang-type term of the corporate world is defined as *a small, often isolated department that functions with minimal supervision*, such as an R&D department, and came from the name of an illicit distillery in Al Capp's comic strip *Li'l Abner*?

29. **QUOTATIONS** What form of speech did American journalist Hugh Rawson say reflects "*a society's outward and visible signs of ... (its) inward anxieties, conflicts, fears, and shames*"?

30. **SLANG** During the 19th century, which of these terms did British philosopher John Stuart Mill call *"a vile specimen of bad English"* after it was used for the first time to mean *to happen*?
    a. occur
    b. transpire
    c. take place

ANSWERS
GAME 7

GAME 7—Level I—1 Point Each

1. titanic
2. a—lily-livered
3. pig
4. nitrates
5. sombrero

GAME 7—Level II—2 Points Each

6. True
7. eddy
8. c—vamoose, which came Spanish *vamos* (let's go)
9. *S*ecurities and *E*xchange *C*ommission
10. sour grapes

GAME 7—Level III—3 Points Each

11. b—road rash
12. buffet / buffet
13. c—German & Japanese
14. à la carte
15. a—the living

GAME 7—Level IV—4 Points Each

16. zero
17. c—scientist, per Otto Jespersen in *Growth and Structure of the*

English Language, 1905
18. peaceful (or friendly) coexistence
19. milkman
20. Murphy's Law—which posits: *anything that can go wrong, will*

GAME 7—Level V—5 Points Each

21. *gnarled* appeared in 1603; *gnarl* was not back-formed until 1814
22. a—46% required knowledge of English
23. a—it is too young and feminine for war news
24. America's NBC. The BBC settled on a geographically limited norm defined as *Southern Received English as taught at Oxford and Cambridge.*
25. weird—The Norns were also known as *The Three Weird Sisters*

GAME 7—Level VI—6 Points Each

26. a—make some money
27. lingua franca
28. skunk works—from Capp's *Skonk Works*
29. euphemism
30. b—transpire, which, until then, was used to mean *to give off vaporous material*

BETHUMP'D REGULAR
GAME 8

GAME 8—LEVEL I

1. **WORD ORIGINS** What name for *a subdivision of a stem* originated in the Latin word for *paw*?

2. **LETTER WORDS** What is meant by the letter word used in this sentence: *"When you drive my car, I want you to treat it with TLC"*?

3. **EPONYMS** In 1881, what word appeared in English as a result of research performed by French chemist Louis Pasteur on the partial sterilization of liquids?

4. **SLANG** According to the spelling of the word, does a *hare-brained* person have the brain power of a rabbit or a scope of vision equal to the width of a hair?

5. **HOMOPHONES** When the butcher's meat scale blew its fuses, she sighed, looked at her impatient customer, and said, *"I'm sorry, mister, but you'll just have to ___ a few minutes for the ___."*

GAME 8— LEVEL II

6. **TRUE OR FALSE** Historically, it is evident that cultural pride has caused the first U.S.-born children of immigrants to speak the language of their ancestors and delay or even refuse

adoption of American English.

7. **EPONYMS** What Brazilian flower was named some time around 1820 in honor of 18th century German botanist B.P. Gloxin?

8. **SLANG** In 1792, what slang term for *jail* appeared in English as a derivative of the Spanish word that is spelled *c-a-l-a-b-o-z-o* and means *dungeon*?

9. **EPONYMS** What colloquial synonym of *huge* and *enormous* came into being after P.T. Barnum bought a baby elephant from the London Zoo for his circus in 1884 and subsequently popularized its name?

10. **GLOBAL ENGLISH** In the 20th century, which of these countries' youth culture, science, and commerce were the dominant factors involved in English's growth to the status of Global Language?
    a. Australia's
    b. Britain's
    c. Canada's
    d. United States'

GAME 8—LEVEL III

11. **BORROWED WORDS** In 1634, what name for a *noisy Australasian crested parrot* came from the Malay word that is phonetically spelled *k-a-k-a-t-u-a*?

12. **WORD ORIGINS** The word *atom* originated in the Greek word *atomos*, which has which of the following meanings?
    a. of or related to Adam
    b. tiny
    c. indivisible

13. **BORROWED WORDS** What word is defined as *exaggera-*

tion by the ludicrous distortion of characteristics and, in 1712, came into English from the Italian word that literally means *act of loading* and is spelled *c-a-r-r-i-c-a-r-e*?

14. PORTMANTEAU WORDS In June 1997, what word that is a blend of the words *racism* and *erase* was used by President Bill Clinton at the University of California in San Diego in a commencement address devoted to the status of race in America?

15. NAMES / NICKNAMES In 1682, what name was used for *those, usually boys, who carried gunpowder from a ship's magazine to the gun deck or cannons*?

    a. idiots
    b. red necks
    c. powder monkeys

GAME 8—LEVEL IV

16. ACRONYMS What act of Congress gave U.S. citizens better access to government documents and other information and is known by the acronym *FOIA*?

17. ACCENTS Though many speakers of American English pronounce the alphabet's twenty-third letter something like *duh-ba-ya*, it is likely their pronunciation would be more accurate if they remembered that the letter was originally derived from the doubled form of what other letter?

18. GLOBAL ENGLISH In Italy, the urge to exploit what linguists call *"the prestige of English"* often leads to naive usages, such as the use of which of the following as the commercial name for *an apple juice drink*?

    a. Apply
    b. Apple Blood
    c. Appear

19. NAMES / NICKNAMES What is the origin of football commentator Pat Summerall's first name?

   a. it's a shortened form of *Patricia*

   b. it's an allusion to his characteristically '*pat*' responses to controversial plays

   c. it's an acronym for *p*oints *a*fter *t*ouchdown

20. HOMONYMS What homonyms evolved from the Dutch word that is spelled *n-e-g-g-e* and means *small horse* and the Old Norse word that is spelled *g-n-a-g-a-n* and means *to gnaw*?

GAME 8—LEVEL V

21. HISTORY Which of these words did the Puritans attempt to ban from use: crucifix, Savior, or Christmas?

22. IDIOMS Idiomatically speaking, is a *four-flusher* an inefficient loo, a bluffer, or an extremely embarrassing incident?

23. HOMOPHONES Identify and spell the homophones defined as:

   a. a virus-caused horny projection from the skin

   b. a liquid from hot soaked mash that is fermented to make beer

24. PIDGINS & CREOLES In the Malay language, which uses reduplicatives to express plurality, if *budak* means *child* what term is used to mean *children*?

25. BORROWED WORDS In 1610, English borrowed the word *opossum* from the Algonquin Indian language where it has which of the following definitions?

   a. white animal

   b. big rat with pocket

   c. sleep faker

GAME 8—LEVEL VI

26. GLOBAL ENGLISH In 1714, what four languages were listed in Veneroni's *Imperial Dictionary* as the chief languages of Europe?
   a. French, German, Italian, Latin
   b. English, French, German, Italian
   c. English, French, Portuguese, Spanish

27. WORD EVOLUTIONS The continuing and accelerating de-Latinization of English is evident in the writing of the plurals of such words as *cactus* and *referendum* as *cactuses* and *referendums* instead of what Latin forms?

28. SLANG What hyphenated synonym of *jitters* and *creeps*, as in "*He has the jitters*," was coined in 1923 by American cartoonist Billy DeBeck?

29. ACCENTS What word gained formal status in 1816 despite having originated as a peculiar or dialectical pronunciation of the word *ordinary*, and is now defined as *having an irritable or cantankerous disposition*?

30. EPONYMS What word is derived from the name of Greek mythological mother of the Muses and goddess of memory, which is spelled *M-n-e-m-o-s-y-n-e*?

GAME 8

GAME 8—Level I—1 Point Each

1. branch—from the Latin *branca*
2. *Tender Loving Care*
3. pasteurize
4. the brain power of a rabbit. Based on the appearance of the term in English, such types were first noticed around 1534.
5. wait / weight

GAME 8—Level II—2 Points Each

6. False—historically, a host of social factors, the most important of which is economic opportunity, encouraged first-generation Americans to adopt American English very quickly, at the expense of their parents' language
7. gloxinia
8. calaboose
9. jumbo—Baby Jumbo grew to be the largest elephant ever known, according to Barnum's publicity, and thereby inserted his name into English's stack of synonyms for *size large*.
10. d—United States'

GAME 8—Level III—3 Points Each

11. cockatoo
12. c—indivisible, but, since the atom is now known to be quite divisible, the name is a misnomer
13. caricature

14. eracism
15. c—powder monkeys

GAME 8—Level IV—4 Points Each

16. *F*reedom *O*f *I*nformation *A*ct
17. u—thence, a pronunciation closer to *"double-u"*
18. a—Apply
19. c—it's an acronym for *points after touchdown*. Born George Allan Summerall, "Pat" was given the nickname when he played professional football and kicked *points after touchdown*.
20. nag / nag

GAME 8—Level V—5 Points Each

21. Christmas—which the Puritans attempted to displace with *Christtide* in order to avoid use of the decidedly Roman Catholic suffix *-mas*
22. a bluffer—the term came from the poker players who continue to bet while holding four cards of the same suit despite knowing that five are needed to win
23. *w-a-r-t* / *w-o-r-t*
24. budak-budak
25. a—white animal

GAME 8—Level VI—6 Points Each

26. a—French, German, Italian, Latin. The use of English in Europe was largely insignificant until the 20th century.
27. cacti / referenda
28. heebie-jeebies
29. ornery
30. mnemonic—which means *assisting memory*

BETHUMP'D REGULAR
GAME 9

GAME 9—LEVEL I

1. **WORD ORIGINS** What word that appeared in English in 1841 came from the Greek words that mean *terrifying lizard* and are spelled *d-e-i-n-o-s* and *s-a-u-r-o-s*?

2. **AMERICANISMS** What form of entertainment contributed these American idioms to the English language: *anti-up, call their bluff, stack the deck*?

3. **IDIOMS** What single word completes these idiomatic statements?
   a. "I'm finished, so ___ me out"
   b. "It's a raw ___."

4. **NAMES / NICKNAMES** In the late 1800s, what sport got its name because its inventor, James Naismith of Springfield, Massachusetts, happen to use peach baskets for goals?

5. **WORD EVOLUTIONS** What steak's name was once defined as *a house that sells malt liquor as porter*?

GAME 9—LEVEL II

6. **NAMES / NICKNAMES** What musical instrument is sometimes referred to as *a licorice stick*?

7. **PHONETICS** Phonetically speaking, what is held in common by the words *knock, gnat,* and *wreath?*

8. **EPONYMS** In 1872, what *element that exists as a colorless nonflammable gas* was named after Helios, Greek god of the sun?

9. **HOMONYMS** Identify the homonyms in this sentence: *A leg-banded ___ from Capistrano made the fat little monk ___ his pride when it returned ten days later than he'd predicted.*

10. **WORD EVOLUTIONS** What word evolved into being due to the chronic mispronunciation of the Middle English word that is spelled *s-h-a-m-e-f-a-s-t* and defined as *rooted in shame?*

GAME 9—LEVEL III

11. **DINOSAUR WORDS** Which of the following is the definition of the now archaic word *ugsome?*
    a. handsome
    b. loathsome
    c. homely

12. **HOMONYMS** What slang-type word that means *bag* or *sack* was borrowed from Old North French in the 13th century and, in the 14th century, became a homonym of another slang-type word akin to a Middle Dutch word that means *to prod* or *to jab?*

13. **HISTORY** In Britain, especially during the reign of Queen Victoria, which of the following became an important determinant of social status?
    a. accent
    b. wealth
    c. education

14. WORD ORIGINS What sequence of four months has names derived from Latin words for numbers that, if used, would position each of the four months two-months earlier in the year?

15. SEXIST ENGLISH What is the gender-neutral version of *suffragette*, a facetious term coined in 1906 in mockery of females who advocate the rights of women?

GAME 9—LEVEL IV

16. WORD ORIGINS The word *infantry* appeared in English in 1579 and originated in the Latin word *infans*, which has which of the following meanings?
   a. young and incapable of speech
   b. small and insignificant
   c. not fancy

17. PIDGINS & CREOLES What is the literal translation of the name of the English-based creole that has become a national language of Papua New Guinea and was formalized in 1974 with the spelling *T-o-k P-i-s-i-n*?

18. HISTORY In 1996, the importation of what type of food products was declared illegal by Quebec's language cops because the labels were not written in French?
   a. kosher
   b. oriental
   c. Mexican

19. HOMOGRAPHS Identify the homographs defined as:
   a. a former monetary unit and coin of Spain
   b. not artificial, fraudulent, or illusory

20. EUPHEMISMS In 1982, what euphemistic term was coined by the corporate world for *the act of reducing costs by elimi-nating inside workers whose tasks are more profitably per-*

formed by outside or foreign contractors?

GAME 9—LEVEL V

21. QUOTATIONS In 1995, which of these politicians declared: *"We must stop the practice of multilingual education as a means of instilling ethnic pride... '"*?
   a. Jesse Helms
   b. Robert Dole
   c. Newt Gingrich

22. PIDGINS & CREOLES In 1985, what did Ken Saro-Wiwa call the language he described in a novel as *"a mixture of Pidgin English, broken English, and occasional flashes of good, even idiomatic English"*?
   a. Ebonics
   b. Semi-English
   c. Rotten English

23. AUSTRALIANISMS In Australia, what is an *offsider*?
   a. a motorcycle sidecar
   b. a companion
   c. a left-handed person

24. EPONYMS What word that is defined as *foolishly impractical* evolved out of the early 17th century chivalric satire by Miguel de Cervantes Saavedra entitled *Don Quixote del la Mancha, El ingenioso hidalgo*?

25. BORROWED WORDS What name for a toy is thought to be from a language of the Phillipines and might be 'loosely' defined as *a reduplicative of a 15th century interjection that many in the 20th century associate with Sylvester Stallone*?

GAME 9—LEVEL VI

26. HOMONYMS Identify the homonyms defined as:

a. various
b. those who remain under water for long periods

27. WORD ORIGINS What word is defined as *overly zealous* and came into English in China in 1942 from Marine Lt. Col. Evans Carlson's misinterpretation of the abbreviated name for the Chinese Industrial Cooperative Society, which is phonetically spelled *g-o-n-g-h-e*?

28. BORROWED WORDS What word defined as *a foreigner who has difficulty speaking intelligible Spanish* came from the Spanish expression *hablar en griego*, which means *to speak in Greek* and is an idiom with the same roots as the English idiom *It's Greek to me*?

29. LINGUISTICS What word of particular importance to lexicographers evolved out of a Greek word that means *the true meaning of a word*?

30. NAMES / NICKNAMES What name for a type of school started out in the 14th century defined as *a secondary school that teaches Latin and Greek in preparation for college*?

ANSWERS

GAME 9

GAME 9—Level I—1 Point Each

1. dinosaur
2. card games—especially poker
3. deal—each use arose from the jargon of card games, especially poker
4. basketball
5. porterhouse

GAME 9—Level II—2 Points Each

6. clarinet
7. the first letter of each is silent
8. helium
9. swallow / swallow
10. shame*faced*

GAME 9—Level III—3 Points Each

11. b—loathsome
12. poke
13. a—accent
14. September (7th month), October (8th month), November (9th month), December (10th month)
15. suffragist

GAME 9—Level IV—4 Points Each

16. a—young and incapable of speech
17. Talk Pidgin or Pidgin Talk
18. a—kosher
19. real / real
20. outsourcing

GAME 9—Level V—5 Points Each

21. b—Robert Dole, presidential candidate, in a Labor Day address at the American Legion convention
22. c—Rotten English, which appears in Saro-Wiwa's novel *Sozaboy* (Soldier Boy)
23. b—a companion
24. quixotic
25. yo-yo, which appeared in English in 1915

GAME 9—Level VI—6 Points Each

26. divers / divers
27. gung-ho
28. gringo
29. etymology—the accepted definition of which, interestingly, implies that if the original meaning of a word is the "true meaning" any changes in meaning must represent forms of degeneration. Hence, we have the notion that language is in a state of continuing decay, a belief that ignores our very obviously improving ability to communicate with precision and accuracy.
30. grammar school

BETHUMP'D REGULAR
GAME 10

GAME 10—LEVEL I

1. **NAMES / NICKNAMES** What South American river's name came from that of a race of female warriors out of Greek mythology?

2. **WORD ORIGINS** What word appeared in English in 1609 that originated in the Greek word spelled *b-a-r-y-t-o-n-o-s*, which means *deep sounding*?

3. **BRITICISMS** In Britain, does a person who works *all the hours God sends* work only on Sundays, only in sunlight, or all the time?

4. **WORD ORIGINS** The Greek word spelled *e-l-a-p-h-o-s*, which means *deer*, is thought to be the root of English's *elk*, while the Greek word spelled *e-l-e-p-h-a-s* is the more certain root of English's name for what other animal?

5. **BORROWED WORDS** In 1751, what word appeared in English as an anglicized version of the French word for *kettle contents*, which is spelled *c-h-a-u-d-i-è-r-e*?

GAME 10—LEVEL II

6. **SLANG** Which of these terms is used by American students as a generic name for *courses designed for those who get into*

college while lacking fundamental skills?
- a. meathead
- b. bonehead
- c. butthead

7. **HOMONYMS** Identify the homonyms defined as:
   - a. the player positioned between guard and end
   - b. equipment used for fishing

8. **BORROWED WORDS** What vegetable's name appeared in English in 1799 as a combination of a Swedish dialect's words for *root*, which is spelled *r-o-t*, and *bag*, which is spelled *b-a-g-g-e*?

9. **EPONYMS** What type of clock got its name from the title of a song published in 1876 by American Henry C. Work?

10. **LETTER WORDS** What letter in the letter word *IOU* is used *only* because of its homophonic character?

GAME 10—LEVEL III

11. **SLANG** When *stumblebum* appeared in English in 1932 its initial use was primarily for inept participants of what sport?

12. **BRITICISMS** Although the British and American pronunciations are similar, how do most British spell the word that most Americans spell *d-r-a-f-t*?

13. **BORROWED WORDS** What name for *a dish that features bits of raw fish or shellfish* was borrowed from Japanese in 1893?

14. **WORD EVOLUTIONS** Which was first to appear in English, *hyper* or *hyperactive*?

15. **NAMES / NICKNAMES** What title of a 1991 novel by

Douglas Coupland is now used as a generic name for *the population wave that is made up of those born between 1965 and 1977?*

GAME 10—LEVEL IV

16. EPONYMS What is the family name of William ___ who, in Virginia during the 1780s, ignored due process of law and used hanging as his preferred means of dispensing justice as he led a self-appointed tribunal of vigilantes to pursue a band of ruffians which had eluded civil authorities?

17. WORD ORIGINS The word *virus* was borrowed intact from Latin in 1599 where it has which of the following meanings?
   a. venom
   b. manly
   c. virtue

18. GLOBAL ENGLISH In December 1995, France's president Jacques Chirac issued a formal warning to 47 French-speaking nations about what new English-based threat to the French language?
   a. the U.S. presence in Bosnia
   b. the Internet
   c. the sudden solidarity of the English-speaking nations opposed to France's nuclear testing program

19. HOMOGRAPHS Identify the homographs defined as:
   a. a standard of personal behavior based on moral principles
   b. to lead or direct

20. HISTORY If *superman* appeared in English in 1903, in which of these years did *superwoman* appear with the definition *an exceptional woman, especially a woman who succeeds in having a career and raising a family?*
   a. 1906

b. 1946

c. 1986

GAME 10—LEVEL V

21. **WORD ORIGINS** What word evolved out of the ancient Greek practice of meeting once a year to decide which trouble-maker in Athens should be temporarily expelled for the good of the city, with the names of candidates submitted on potsherds or shells called *ostrakon*?

22. **WORD EVOLUTIONS** What word has Latin roots that mean *greyish or blue*, evolved to become a synonym of the condition *black-and-blue*, evolved further to *ashen* and *pallid*, and, as a synonym of *enraged*, is now defined as *red with anger*?

23. **PORTMANTEAU WORDS** In 1979, what word was coined with facetious intent but was quickly adopted for serious intent after a former live-in lover successfully sued an actor for support?

24. **WORD ORIGINS** What Japanese word literally means *divine wind* and originated in Japan in 1274 after the violent winds of a sudden storm destroyed the invading fleet of Mongol leader Kubilai Khan?
    a. banzai
    b. kamikaze
    c. sushi

25. **ACCENTS** In WW II, which of these was a key reason why the British Ministry of Information selected Northumbrian Wilfred Pickles as a BBC newsreader?
    a. he spoke with crisp clarity
    b. in the dark of war, his accent was entertaining
    c. German saboteurs would find his accent hard to imitate

GAME 10—LEVEL VI

26. GLOBAL ENGLISH In Germany, when words appear in ads that, for example, are spelled *c-l-u-b*, *c-r-e-a-t-i-v*, and *e-x-c-l-u-s-i-v*, why is it evident German advertisers are striving for an English appearance?

27. HOMOPHONES When homophone pairs are used by a speaker, what is vital to determining which of each pair is used?

28. BORROWED WORDS Which of the following is the literal Spanish meaning of *bonanza*, a word that was borrowed in 1844 and used in American miners' jargon to mean *an exceptionally large and rich mineral deposit*?
  a. calm sea
  b. big boned
  c. good veins

29. EPONYMS What potent liquor is redistilled from pulque, the alcohol made from the fermented sap of various agaves, and is named after a town in Jalisco, Mexico?

30. HISTORY Who introduced the idea that *all languages are degenerating or following a slow state of decline from erstwhile perfection*?
  a. the Stoics, 2,400 years ago
  b. Francis Bacon, in the 16th century
  c. George Bernard Shaw, in the 20th century

ANSWERS
GAME 10

GAME 10—Level I—1 Point Each

1. Amazon
2. baritone
3. all the time
4. elephant
5. chowder

GAME 10—Level II—2 Points Each

6. b—bonehead, a term that appeared in 1917 in usages like *bonehead* English, *bonehead* algebra, and others
7. tackle / tackle
8. rutabaga
9. grandfather clock—from Work's song *My Grandfather's Clock*
10. the U—which is a homophone of *y-o-u*. *O* is a homophone of *owe*, but it's also the word's first letter.

GAME 10—Level III—3 Points Each

11. boxing
12. *d-r-a-u-g-h-t*
13. sushi
14. *hyperactive* appeared in 1867; *hyper* was not back-formed until 1971
15. *Generation X*

GAME 10—Level IV—4 Points Each

16. Lynch—from which came *lynch law* and, in 1836, the first use of *lynch* as a verb
17. a—venom
18. b—the Internet
19. conduct / conduct
20. a—1906

GAME 10—Level V—5 Points Each

21. ostracize
22. livid—from the Latin *livere*
23. palimony—from *pal* + *alimony*
24. b—kamikaze
25. c—German saboteurs would find his accent hard to imitate

GAME 10—Level VI—6 Points Each

26. if written in German, each would use *k* instead of *c*
27. context
28. a—calm sea
29. tequila
30. a—the Stoics, 2,400 years ago

GAME 11—LEVEL I

1. **SLANG** In 1981, what term appeared in English defined as *a greeting or congratulatory response that involves the slapping of upraised hands by two people*?

2. **IDIOMS** A statement made with the intent of distracting attention from the real issue is known idiomatically as a *herring* of what color?

3. **HISTORY** Which of these names for colors did *not* appear in English until the late 19th century: black, red, chartreuse, green, orange?

4. **TRUE OR FALSE** Many U.S. publishers believe it is necessary to hire translators to convert the writing of British authors into American English.

5. **EPONYMS** What fruit is a raspberry-blackberry hybrid and in 1935 was named after American horticulturist Rudolph Boysen?

GAME 11— LEVEL II

6. **PORTMANTEAU WORDS** In 1879, what word defined as *slangy speech or writing* appeared in English as a blend of the words *language* and *slang*?

7. **NAMES / NICKNAMES** What name was given to *the explosion of births that occurred soon after the end of World War II?*

8. **HOMOGRAPHS** When his father insisted that a light-weight motorbike like a ___ was too dangerous for a six-year-old, the youngster sulked and ___ around the house for a week.

9. **HOMOPHONES** The crowd at the track roared with laughter when Seattle Slow sprang out of the ___, lurched to a stop, then trotted on with a swaggering, oddly comical ___.

10. **WORD ORIGINS** Which of these words came from Greek where it has the literal meaning of *one who eats at the table of another?*
    a. neighbor
    b. relative
    c. parasite

GAME 11—LEVEL III

11. **HOMONYMS** What piece of equipment vital to ice hockey has a name that is a homonym of an archaic word that means *an evil spirit* or *a demon?*

12. **BORROWED WORDS** What German word defined as *a war that is conducted with lightning speed and great force* appeared in English in 1939?

13. **HOMOPHONES** Identify and spell the homophones defined as:
    a. water from the condensation of atmospheric vapor
    b. a restraining influence
    c. royal authority

14. IDIOMS Idiomatically speaking, the crossing of which of these rivers commits a person irrevocably to a given course of action?
   a. North America's Mississippi
   b. South America's Amazon
   c. Italy's Rubicon

15. NAMES / NICKNAMES Is a *goatsucker* a snake, bird, or bat?

GAME 11—LEVEL IV

16. BRITICISMS In Britain, what are you being advised to do if someone sidles up and whispers: *"If I were you, luv, I'd scarper'"*?
   a. run away
   b. save your money
   c. down your drink in one gulp

17. TRUE OR FALSE Although it is a common perception, no known professional linguist really believes that language ability is linked to genetics.

18. HISTORY Changing social attitudes explain why those who were known in the early 20th century as *vagrants*, *bums*, and *hoboes* were, by the end of the century, referred to with what more compassionate word?

19. WORD ORIGINS What word do etymologists suspect evolved from the ancient Sanskrit word that means *year* or *season* and is spelled *s-a-m-a*?

20. ACCENTS What is meant if a person from Baltimore makes a two-word statement that sounds as though it should be spelled *"L-e-s-s s-q-u-e-e-t'"*?

GAME 11—LEVEL V

21. BORROWED WORDS After borrowing French words that were spelled *d-e-t-t-e* and *d-o-u-t-e*, what odd-ball thing did the fastidious British eventually do to tidy up and underscore the words' more acceptable Latin roots?

22. BRITICISMS In Britain, which of these is called *the back of a house*?
   a. its rooftop
   b. its front
   c. its foundation

23. WORD EVOLUTIONS What name for a type of publication originated in Arabic and worked its way through Old Provençal and on into Middle French where, in 1583, it was snatched by English and defined as *a warehouse, a place where powder and other explosives are kept*?

24. JARGON The term *yellow journalism* is newspaper jargon for *low grade or sensational journalism* and originated in which of the following?
   a. the brittle yellowing of aged newspaper
   b. the association of yellow with mediocre and cowardly
   c. the toothless Yellow Kid from the comic strip *Hogan's Alley,* by Joseph Pulitzer

25. GLOBAL ENGLISH For what reason in 1983 did the nomadic African tribe, the Tuareg, delay by ten days its annual migration to fresh pastures?
   a. to show off their English to Queen Elizabeth
   b. to watch the last episode of U.S. TV's *Dallas*
   c. they heard and understood an English-speaking radio announcer predict a major flood

GAME 11—LEVEL VI

26. BRITICISMS What should you do if a London Cockney says, *"Matey, you'd best zhoosh your riah"*?
   a. get moving, work faster
   b. fix your hair
   c. shut your mouth, be quiet

27. EPONYMS What is the family name of Colonel Jean ___, the 17th century drill master and stiff-backed disciplinarian who taught the army of Louis XIV to march toward the enemy in line formations and shoot in volleys only on command?

28. WORD EVOLUTIONS What was the definition of the word *condominium* when it appeared in English around 1714?
   a. containing (the) huddled masses
   b. within God's domain
   c. the joint sovereignty of two or more nations

29. HISTORY In 1981, which of these U.S. senators proposed an amendment to the Constitution to make English the official language of the United States?
   a. Robert Dole
   b. Jesse Helms
   c. Samuel Hayakawa

30. GENERAL QUESTIONS Since none of the member states of the European Free Trade Association—Austria, Finland, Iceland, Norway, Sweden, Switzerland—are native speakers of English, in 1990 what language was declared its official language?

ANSWERS
GAME 11

GAME 11—Level I—1 Point Each

1. high five
2. red—the use of the term in this context came from the practice of dragging an odoriferous red herring across a trail to confuse scent-pursuing hunting dogs
3. chartreuse—which appeared in 1884
4. True
5. boysenberry

GAME 11—Level II—2 Points Each

6. slanguage
7. baby boom—which actually appeared in English in 1941 in response to what was clearly predictable
8. moped / moped
9. gate / gait
10. c—parasite, from *para* (beside) + *sitos* (food)

GAME 11—Level III—3 Points Each

11. puck
12. blitzkrieg
13. *r-a-i-n* / *r-e-i-n* / *r-e-i-g-n*
14. Italy's Rubicon—whose crossing by Julius Caesar in 49 B.C.E. was declared an act of war by Rome's senate
15. bird—which is nocturnal, eats insects, does not suck on goats, and is also known as a *nightjar*

GAME 11—Level IV—4 Points Each

16. a—run away
17. False—for example, see the work of American linguist Noam Chomsky. Such opinions of professional linguists led to the listing of genetics as a key factor in the Oakland, California School District's resolution to formalize Ebonics.
18. homeless—a term that has been in the language since at least 1615
19. summer
20. "Let's go eat."

GAME 11—Level V—5 Points Each

21. they inserted a quite useless *silent b* (and altered the spellings) to produce *debt* and *doubt*
22. a—its rooftop
23. magazine
24. c—the toothless Yellow Kid from the comic strip *Hogan's Alley*, by Joseph Pulitzer
25. b—to watch the last episode of U.S. TV's *Dallas*

GAME 11—Level VI—6 Points Each

26. b—fix your hair
27. Martinet
28. c—the joint sovereignty of two or more nations
29. c—Samuel Hayakawa, who, when the attempt failed, co-founded the pro-English organization called *U.S. English*
30. English

BETHUMP'D REGULAR
GAME 12

GAME 12—LEVEL I

1. **WORD ORIGINS** What disease's name came from the Latin word that means *madness, to rave* and is spelled *r-a-b-e-r-e*?

2. **IDIOMS** When is *dribbling all around the floor* an accepted form of behavior?

3. **WORD ORIGINS** Did *prom*, the name for *a formal high school or college dance*, come from a shortened form of promise, prominent, or promenade?

4. **BRITICISMS** In Britain, is a *quid* a baby quail, a pound sterling, or a type of fish?

5. **WORD EVOLUTIONS** What word that means *little stone* was spelled *p-a-p-o-l-s-t-a-n* in Old English and *p-o-p-p-l-e* in Middle English?

GAME 12—LEVEL II

6. **GRAMMAR** Which shows less variation, written English or spoken English?

7. **IDIOMS** Which of the following is the correct interpretation of the statement *"He eats like a bird"*?
   a. he gulps and swallows food whole

b. he eats roadkill, like a buzzard or crow

c. he doesn't eat very much

8. **EPONYMS** Who among the following is memorialized by the *Edgar*, the prize awarded annually for notable achievement in mystery writing?

    a. J. Edgar Hoover

    b. Edgar Allan Poe

    c. Edgar Bergen

9. **SLANG** In 1981, what term appeared in English as an altered form of the phrase *want to be* and is now defined as *a person who tries to look or act like someone else*?

10. **WORD ORIGINS** Spell the word that originated in and evolved out of the Latin word *supersaltus*, which has the literal meaning of *over leap*.

GAME 12—LEVEL III

11. **EUPHEMISMS** What is a clearer and more direct way of wording a sign that says, *"Do Not Expectorate"*?

12. **BORROWED WORDS** What word that was spelled c-r-o-y-n-e-n in Middle English came from the Dutch word for *to chatter* and is often associated with the singing style of Frank Sinatra?

13. **WORD EVOLUTIONS** What slang-sounding word is defined as *a special domain*, and is a holdover from 15th century Middle English when it was defined as *the dwelling place of a bailiff*?

14. **BRITICISMS** What do the British use as *a generic name for barley, wheat, oats, rye, and other cereal grains*?

    a. corn

    b. maize

c. mash

15. NAMES / NICKNAMES . Are *the children of post-World War II baby boomers* known by columnists and others in the news media as boomer babies, boom-boomers, or echo boomers?

GAME 12—LEVEL IV

16. LETTER WORDS In 1968, what letter-number word came into English from the Russian term that is spelled and numbered *a-v-t-o-m-a-t K-a-l-a-s-h-n-i-k-o-v-a 1947*?

17. WORD ORIGINS What political movement was founded by Benito Mussolini in 1919 and given a name derived from that of *a cylindrical bundle of rods*, such as the one seen on the obverse side of the U.S. dime, which in Ancient Rome served as a symbol of unity and authority and is spelled *f-a-s-c-i-s*?

18. EPONYMS In 1782, what name was coined by Swedish chemist Torbern Olof Bergman for the chemical the ancients once made by combining sea salt with the camels' urine that was scooped from a cesspool near the temple of the Egyptian god whose name is spelled *A-m-m-o-n*?

19. NAMES / NICKNAMES What was Washington Irving saying about New York City when he dubbed it *Gotham*?
    a. it is the U.S. center for Gothic architecture
    b. it is dominated by Teutonic thinking
    c. it is populated by fools

20. GLOBAL ENGLISH What term from the U.S. corporate world appeared in 1960 defined as *a generous severance package that is designed to induce early retirement*, and was borrowed by Dutch where it is spelled *g-o-u-d-e-n h-a-n-d-d-r-u-c-k*?

GAME 12—LEVEL V

21. HOMOPHONES Identify and spell the homophones defined as:
   a. an incrustation of frost
   b. to correspond in sound

22. QUOTATIONS Was Alexis de Tocqueville referring to someone from Australia, Britain, Canada, or the United States when he wrote: *"An ___ cannot converse, but he can discuss, and his talk falls into a dissertation. He speaks to you as if he was addressing a meeting ..."*?

23. ACRONYMS What is meant by the acronym *GATT*?

24. EPONYMS The word *nemesis* came directly from the name of the goddess Nemesis, who, according to the ancient Greeks, oversees which of the following?
   a. the coining of names
   b. retributive justice and vengeance
   c. the proliferation of nematodes

25. SEXIST ENGLISH When writing, what word is increasingly used to avoid the sexist use of *he* or the clumsy alternating use of *he-she* and *she-he*, even though it violates what tradition-bound grammarians call 'number concord'?

GAME 12—LEVEL VI

26. EUPHEMISMS Which of the following was awarded the National Council of Teachers of English's Doublespeak Award after referring to the neutron bomb as *"a radiation enhancement weapon"*?
   a. the Pentagon
   b. Edward Teller
   c. Westinghouse Corporation

27. HISTORY In 1702, what then-unique concept did lexicographer John Kersey introduce as the purpose of dictionaries?
   a. to inventory the definitions of all exotic words
   b. to adhere to and promote Oxford spellings
   c. to inventory the definitions of all words

28. AUSTRALIANISMS Which of these is known as a *polony* in West Australia, a *devon* in New South Wales, and a *fritz* in South Australia?
   a. a carbonated drink
   b. a sausage
   c. a ram lamb

29. WORD ORIGINS The word *noon* came from the Latin word *nonus* and, thus, was originally used to designate what hour after sunrise?

30. QUOTATIONS Who defined *prose* as *"words in their best order"* and *poetry* as *"the best words in the best order"*?
   a. Samuel Coleridge (1772-1834)
   b. Mary Ann Evans (1819-1880)
   c. Robert Frost (1874-1963)

ANSWERS

GAME 12

GAME 12—Level I—1 Point Each

1. rabies—which appeared in English around 1598
2. when playing basketball
3. promenade—*prom* appeared in English around 1894
4. a pound sterling
5. pebble

GAME 12—Level II—2 Points Each

6. written English—which, when compared to spoken English, usually does not reveal dialectical and related speech patterns, and is done in a formal style that lies within the constraints of learned rules of grammar
7. c—he doesn't eat very much
8. b—Edgar Allen Poe, who is called *"The father of the detective story"*
9. wanna-be or wannabe
10. *s-o-m-e-r-s-a-u-l-t*—which English borrowed from French sometime around 1530

GAME 12—Level III—3 Points Each

11. "Don't Spit"
12. croon
13. bailiwick
14. a—corn. The British use *maize* when they mean *corn*.
15. echo boomers

GAME 12—Level IV—4 Points Each

16. AK-47—which is a 7.62 mm rifle designed by the Soviets
17. fascism
18. ammonia
19. c—it is populated by fools, which is an equating Irving apparently made with the story of Gotham, England whose citizens diverted a visit by hated King John by acting like fools and madmen, thereby suggesting that a dangerous contagion had struck the town
20. golden handshake

GAME 12—Level V—5 Points Each

21. *r-i-m-e* / *r-h-y-m-e*
22. United States—from de Tocqueville's *Democracy in America* (1835)
23. *G*eneral *A*greement on *T*ariffs and *T*rade
24. b—retributive justice and vengeance
25. they

GAME 12—Level VI—6 Points Each

26. a—the Pentagon
27. c—to inventory the definitions of all words. Until Kersey, dictionaries were mostly compilations limited to difficult or, as then expressed, *"hard visuall words,"* under the assumption that there was no need to document common or everyday terms. Kersey's concept, however, was largely ignored until later that century when Samuel Johnson put it into practice.
28. b—a sausage
29. ninth—about three o'clock
30. a—Samuel Coleridge (1772-1834)

BETHUMP'D REGULAR
GAME 13

GAME 13—LEVEL I

1. **EPONYMS** In 1893, what device was named after American engineer George Washington Gale Ferris?

2. **SLANG** What slang term appeared in English in 1971 as a shortened form of the word *suburbs*?

3. **IDIOMS** Which of these animal's enthusiasm and work ethic is frequently alluded to in idiomatic expressions: buffalo, bear, bull, or beaver?

4. **BORROWED WORDS** In the wild and woolly American west of the 1850s, what Mexican-Spanish word that means *rough and wild* was borrowed into English as a term for *an unbroken horse*?

5. **WORD ORIGINS** What word was borrowed into English from French in the 14th century that originated in the Latin word *carpentarius*, which means *carriage maker*?

GAME 13—LEVEL II

6. **ACRONYMS** In 1945, what acronym was coined for the technical term *sound navigation ranging*?

7. **PORTMANTEAU WORDS** In 1940, what word that is

defined as *the beautiful people* was formed by blending the words *literati* and *glitter*?

8. **HOMOPHONES** When an angry bull roared into the garden, the pumpkin, terrified, nudged the zucchini and whispered: *"Don't move a leaf, Zucci, or you'll be a squashed squash and I'll be a ___ ___."*

9. **EPONYMS** In 1756, which of the following was named after Marquise de Pompadour?
   a. a front-mounded hair style
   b. Pompano Beach, Florida
   c. the musical piece *Pomp and Circumstance*

10. **SEXIST ENGLISH** Which of these, due to traditional usage, connotes an activity limited to females?
    a. pool party
    b. slumber party
    c. house party

GAME 13—LEVEL III

11. **CANADIANISMS** What does a Canadian mean when he says, *"I booked off today"*?
    a. he told his employer he's not reporting for work
    b. he did not place bets with his bookie
    c. he succumbed to a reading frenzy at a library

12. **BRITICISMS** In Britain, is a *merrythought* a get-well card, a fleeting vicarious vision, or the wishbone of a chicken?

13. **HISTORY** In 1961, Congress passed a resolution identifying Samuel Wilson, the military's beef supplier during the War of 1812, as the namesake of what character who symbolizes the United States and the American people?

14. **WORD EVOLUTIONS** In Old English, what words were

spelled *m-e-l-k-e*, *w-u-l-f-a-s*, and *b-u-t-e-r-e*?

15. **NAMES / NICKNAMES** In 1840, what alternate name for a prominence on the elbow was coined as a pun on the formal anatomical name for the long bone of the upper arm, which is spelled *h-u-m-e-r-u-s*?

GAME 13—LEVEL IV

16. **EPONYMS** What tree preserves the Middle English name for *Prussia*, which was once a major supplier of the long, straight conifer logs that were prized for their value as ship masts?
   a. pine
   b. cedar
   c. spruce

17. **CANADIANISMS** In the wide wind-swept prairies of western Canada, what is a *Calgary Redeye*?
   a. a fundamentalist's fiery sermon
   b. an around-the-clock wheat harvesting session
   c. a beer mixed with tomato juice

18. **QUOTATIONS** On October 30, 1995, what U.S. congressional leader proclaimed: *"Allowing bilingualism to continue is very dangerous. We should insist on English as a common language. ...That's what binds us together"*?

19. **WORD EVOLUTIONS** Which of the following words appeared in English during the 15th century defined as *to divert attention so as to deceive*, evolved to mean *to absorb* then, later, *to distract or bewilder*, and is now defined as *to entertain in a light and playful manner*?
   a. kid
   b. josh
   c. amuse

20. EUPHEMISMS During the Vietnam War, Phnom Penh embassy airforce attaché Colonel David Ofgor insisted that reporters use the term *air support* instead of their embarrassing, relentless, and annoying use of what alternate term?
   a. bombings
   b. fly-ins
   c. air lifts

GAME 13—LEVEL V

21. AUSTRALIANISMS In Australia, what is a *snob*?
   a. a sports team captain with a winning record
   b. a cobbler or shoemaker
   c. it's an acronym for *sneaky old bloke*

22. NAMES / NICKNAMES If an *aptronym* is defined as *a name that matches its owner's character, trade, or mission, often in a humorous or ironic way*, which 1996 presidential candidate's name is an aptronym for *an opponent of welfare*?

23. BORROWED WORDS What state is known for its many pristine lakes and has a name that came from a term in the language of the Sioux that means *cloudy water*?

24. IDIOMS A story by which of these authors led to the adoption and widespread use of the idiom *a fool's paradise*?
   a. William Shakespeare
   b. Mark Twain
   c. John Milton

25. GENERAL QUESTIONS If there are about 184,000 words in the common, non-scientific vocabulary of German and 615,000 in English, does French have more than 930,000, about 500,000, or less than 100,000?

GAME 13—LEVEL VI

26. ACCENTS In 1926, when John Reith concluded it was necessary for the BBC to establish a norm for pronunciation, how did he describe the goal?
   a. a style that will not be laughed at in any part of the country
   b. a commercial form of the King's English
   c. a spoken form approved by the House of Lords

27. AUSTRALIANISMS In Australia, what is *plonk*?
   a. plentiful money
   b. cheap wine
   c. plagiarized writing

28. BRITICISMS What do the British call *a private school*?
   a. a public school
   b. a caste academy
   c. a social preparatory

29. WORD ORIGINS Where did the British get the L-symbol (£) they use for their monetary unit, the pound?
   a. the L from Latin's *lucrum*, the root of *lucre*
   b. the L from *Lucifer*, the root of all evil
   c. the L from Latin's *libra*

30. BORROWED WORDS What word that is defined as *to stand in the way of* was borrowed in 1902 from Scottish where it is defined as *to obstruct a golf shot by positioning a ball between the opponent's ball and the cup*?

ANSWERS

GAME 13

GAME 13—Level I—1 Point Each

1. the Ferris wheel
2. burbs—as in "She's from the *burbs* of Jersey."
3. beaver—as in "He's as *busy as a beaver*" and "She's *an eager beaver.*"
4. bronco
5. carpenter—which came into English from the Old North French word *carpentier*

GAME 13—Level II—2 Points Each

6. sonar
7. glitterati
8. gored / gourd
9. a—a front-mounded hair style
10. b—slumber party

GAME 13—Level III—3 Points Each

11. a—he told his employer he's not reporting for work
12. the wishbone of a chicken
13. Uncle Sam—which is how, during his time, the locals in Troy, New York referred to Wilson as well as to his "U.S."-stamped barrels of beef.
14. milk, wolves, butter
15. funny bone

GAME 13—Level IV—4 Points Each

16. c—spruce, which was a Middle English alteration of the Old French name for Prussia, *Pruce*
17. c—a beer mixed with tomato juice
18. Newt Gingrich—Republican, Speaker of the House
19. c—amuse
20. a—bombings, a word that is also known to have rattled embattled President Lyndon Johnson

GAME 13—Level V—5 Points Each

21. b—a cobbler or shoemaker
22. Bob *Dole*
23. Minnesota
24. c—John Milton, in *Paradise Lost* (1667)
25. less than 100,000—which explains, in part, why today's French youth are so quick to borrow words from English

GAME 13—Level VI—6 Points Each

26. a—a style that will not be laughed at in any part of the country
27. b—cheap wine, which, in Australia, is much loved by a *plonko*
28. a—a public school
29. c—the L from Latin's *libra*, which is also the source of the symbol for the pound weight unit, *lb.*
30. stymie

BETHUMP'D REGULAR
GAME 14

GAME 14—LEVEL I

1. **EPONYMS** What month of the year is named after the Roman god of doors, gates, and all beginnings?

2. **IDIOMS** Idiomatically speaking, does *"He's missing a couple spots on his dice"* mean he cheats at gambling, he's cheated at gambling, or he's a bit weird?

3. **SLANG** What do you serve the grumpy dude who straddles a stool at the counter and mumbles: *"Coffee, high test"*?

4. **WORD EVOLUTIONS** Spell the word that evolved out of the word *accord* and is defined as *three or more musical notes played together.*

5. **BORROWED WORDS** What word is defined as *resembling the walking dead* and is thought by etymologists to have come into English from the Kongo word that means *a god* and is phonetically spelled *n-z-a-m-b-i*?

GAME 14—LEVEL II

6. **NAMES / NICKNAMES** What famous baseball great of '98 acquired a nickname that's the same as the name of a famous hamburger?

7. **DINOSAUR WORDS** Which of these doublets cover the original 14th century meaning of the *fell* in the phrase *in one fell swoop*?
   a. fierce, deadly
   b. gentle, easy
   c. fast, quick

8. **EPONYMS** What word is defined as *exposure to imminent loss, injury, or death* and came from the name of a French game that Chaucer spelled *j-u-p-a-r-t-i-e*?

9. **HOMOPHONES** Identify and spell the homophones in: *"After her emotional friend lost a huge trout off his line, she waited with ___ breath as he frantically ___ the hook again."*

10. **SLANG** In about 1971, what term was coined as a name for *hunger pangs* then quickly expanded its repertoire of definitions to include *light snack foods*?

GAME 14—LEVEL III

11. **BORROWED WORDS** If English's more recent borrowings from French are pronounced more French-like, which of these triplets was borrowed first?
   a. champagne, chef, chandelier
   b. charge, change, chief

12. **GENERAL QUESTIONS** Understanding occurs between a speaker and a listener *only* when they:
   a. are from the same generation
   b. speak the same language
   c. attach the same meanings to the words used

13. **HISTORY** Western science's tradition of borrowing words from Arabic, Greek, and Latin began because:
   a. it created an image of worldly enlightenment
   b. the sciences of the Arabs, Greeks, and Romans were

more advanced
c. it protected inventions from charlatans

14. BRITICISMS What is revealed when a London chef glibly says, *"I'm cooking a large Swede for dinner'"*?
a. the chef's Viking ancestry
b. a freudian example of Saxon barbarianism
c. the name the British use for rutabagas

15. PORTMANTEAU WORDS During the period of Middle English what words were blended and later altered to form the word *fortnight*, which is defined as *a period of two weeks*?

GAME 14—LEVEL IV

16. BRITICISMS In Britain, is a *courgette* a sporty English Ford, young French maid, or squash?

17. ACRONYMS What group of language arts educators is known by the acronym *TESOL*?

18. AUSTRALIANISMS Which of the following words did 'A. Marjoribanks' calculate was said no less than 18.2 million times during the adult life of a 70-year-old Australian bullock driver?
a. bloody
b. bully
c. golly

19. ACCENTS What 1913 play by George Bernard Shaw makes the point that in Britain's class-stratified society powerful judgements of a person's worth are based on the person's accent?

20. HISTORY In 1697, Boston clergyman and author Cotton Mather was among if not the first to apply which of these names to English-speaking settlers in the New World?

a. Royalists
b. Yankees
c. Americans

GAME 14—LEVEL V

21. **EPONYMS** Which of the following has a common name that is the root of the word *chubby*?
    a. a fat-cheeked fish
    b. the typically plump chicks of a chukar partridge
    c. a square chunk of blubber

22. **HISTORY** In Britain, whose reign did Thomas Sheridan call *"the golden age of spoken English"*?
    a. Queen Elizabeth I's, who reigned 1558-1603
    b. Queen Anne's, who reigned 1702-1714
    c. Queen Victoria's, who reigned 1837-1901

23. **HOMONYMS** What homonyms did English create in the 14th and 15th centuries when it borrowed and anglicized the Middle French words that are spelled *r-e-i-l-l-e*, which means *ruler*, and *r-a-i-l-l-e-r*, which means *to mock*?

24. **WORD EVOLUTIONS** Although the word that is spelled *c-a-t-a-r-r-h* was in use since the 15th century, what word coined in 1906 by Austrian scientist C.E. von Pirquet displaced it, relatively speaking, almost overnight?
    a. influenza
    b. allergy
    c. virus

25. **SEXIST ENGLISH** Why does the name *George Eliot* serve as strong evidence of the historical male biases of English?

GAME 14—LEVEL VI

26. WORD EVOLUTIONS   In the 18th century, the letter *V* was considered to be the consonant form of the letter *U.*   In what order, then, do these words appear in Samuel Johnson's dictionary: *VEAL, VAULT, UDDER?*

27. BORROWED WORDS   What word that is defined as *a fabricated report* came into English in 1859 from a French idiom for cheating, which is literally translated as *to half-sell ducks?*

28. EPONYMS   What type of newspaper is defined as *an official journal* and got its name from that of the Venetian copper coin that was charged in 1531 when the first of its kind was published and sold?

29. WORD EVOLUTIONS   What word started out in Middle English defined as *cotton padding* and is now more commonly used to mean *overstuffed speech or writing?*

30. GLOBAL ENGLISH   During the 1990s, which of these beliefs motivated the actions of language rights advocate Robert Phillipson of Roskilde University in Denmark?
   a.   language diversity enhances world peace
   b.   the use of English warps the mind
   c.   a cabal of British linguists is conspiring to take over the world

ANSWERS

GAME 14

GAME 14—Level I—1 Point Each

1. January—which came from the name of the Roman god *Janus*
2. he's a bit weird
3. caffeinated coffee
4. *c-h-o-r-d*
5. zombie

GAME 14—Level II—2 Points Each

6. Mark *"Big Mac"* McGwire
7. a—fierce, deadly
8. jeopardy
9. *b-a-t-e-d* / *b-a-i-t-e-d*
10. munchies

GAME 14—Level III—3 Points Each

11. b—charge, change, chief
12. c—attach the same meanings to the words used
13. b—the sciences of the Arabs, Greeks, and Romans were more advanced
14. c—the name the British use for *rutabagas* which, apparently, as far as the British are concerned, all come from Sweden
15. fourteen + night—which in Middle English was spelled *f-o-u-r-t-e-n-i-g-h-t*

GAME 14—Level IV—4 Points Each

16. a squash—especially a zucchini
17. *T*eachers of *E*nglish to *S*peakers of *O*ther *L*anguages
18. a—bloody
19. *Pygmalion*
20. c—Americans, which, previously, was only used when referring to the native peoples and fauna

GAME 14—Level V—5 Points Each

21. a—a fat-cheeked fish, the *chub*
22. b—Queen Anne's, who reigned 1702-1714
23. rail / rail
24. b—allergy
25. it is the pen name Mary Ann Evans (1819-1880), author of *Adam Bede*, used in order to get her work published and read

GAME 14—Level VI—6 Points Each

26. VAULT, UDDER, VEAL
27. canard
28. gazette—from Italian *gazetta*, a penny-like coin
29. bombast
30. b—the use of English warps the mind

BETHUMP'D REGULAR
GAME 15

GAME 15—LEVEL I

1. **SLANG** What *slang term for a five-dollar bill* came from the Yiddish word for *five*, which is spelled *f-i-n-f*?

2. **EPONYMS** In 1931, the name of American cartoonist Rube Goldberg was attached to which of the following?
   a. rubella and rubeola
   b. hicks and other rustics
   c. unnecessarily complex contraptions

3. **NAMES / NICKNAMES** In 1915, what name was given to *a small chemicals-filled bomb that on bursting releases a foul odor*?

4. **BORROWED WORDS** In 1565, what vegetable's name originated in the Taino language of the Greater Antilles and Bahamas and was borrowed into English from the Spanish rendition that is spelled *b-a-t-a-t-a*?

5. **IDIOMS** Idiomatically speaking, do those who say nasty things about their enemies sling slop, guns, or mud?

GAME 15—LEVEL II

6. **WORD ORIGINS** What word originated in the Greek word that means *of hearing*, which is spelled *a-k-o-u-s-t-i-k-o-s*, and

appeared in English in 1605 when Francis Bacon borrowed it for use in his dissertation entitled *Advancement in Learning*?

7. **DINOSAUR WORDS** Is *the biblical distance between the elbow and the tip of the middle finger* known as one cubit, two stones, or three measures?

8. **HOMOPHONES** Identify the homophones defined as:
    a. an ornament worn around the neck
    b. the condition of having no neck

9. **ACCENTS** What is a friend from Philly saying when he greets you with a one syllable utterance that sounds like it should be spelled *S-u-p*?

10. **WORD ORIGINS** What name for a cold dessert originated in the Latin term *perfectus*, has the literal French meaning of *something perfect*, and first appeared in English in 1894?

GAME 15—LEVEL III

11. **PORTMANTEAU WORDS** Identify and spell the word that was coined in 1951 as a blend of the terms *cross-country* and *motorcycle*.

12. **SLANG** Which of these synonyms for *smart aleck* appeared in English in 1904: wisenheimer, Flippant Phil, or Mouthy Mabel?

13. **NAMES / NICKNAMES** Sometime in the late 1970s, what term appeared in English defined as *a person who supervises others with excessive control or attention to details*?
    a. nitpicker
    b. shoulder parrot
    c. micromanager

14. **BORROWED WORDS** In 1893, what term was borrowed

intact from Latin and applied to the diplomas of college students whose performance qualified them to graduate *with praise*?

15. **HISTORY** In which part of the world did the name for the food preparation of hog intestines known as *chitterlings* or *chittlins* originate?
    a. West Africa
    b. southeastern United States
    c. England

GAME 15—LEVEL IV

16. **EPONYMS** In 1899, what name for *a type of riding breeches* came from that of a city in India?

17. **BRITICISMS** Which of these terms do the British use when they refer to *hyphenated surnames*?
    a. double-barreled
    b. combo-nicks
    c. his-and-hers

18. **BORROWED WORDS** Is *penny, nickel, dime,* or *quarter* from a German word that means *goblin*?

19. **WORD ORIGINS** What symbol came into being as a result of the stylistic writing by Medieval scribes of the Latin word that is spelled *e-t*?

20. **HISTORY** Based on historical evidence, what happens every time linguists, philologists, and other language experts classify a newly coined word as *a barbarism*?
    a. nothing
    b. the word disappears from use
    c. curiosty is stimulated and the word often gains immediate popularity

GAME 15—LEVEL V

21. GLOBAL ENGLISH In what year did Frenchman Roland de la Platière predict that American English would one day become the world language: 1789, 1889, or 1989?

22. NAMES / NICKNAMES On November 3, 1969, who publicly used and thus popularized the term *the silent majority*?
   a. Lyndon Johnson
   b. Jerry Falwell
   c. Richard Nixon

23. BORROWED WORDS What movie star likes to use the French word for *me* and often says, with righteous indignation and palpable innocence, *"Who, moi"*?

24. QUOTATIONS Who wrote: *"A living language is like a man suffering incessantly from small hemorrhages, and what it needs above all else is constant (infusions) of new blood from other tongues"*?
   a. George Bernard Shaw
   b. Noah Webster
   c. H.L. Mencken

25. GLOBAL ENGLISH To counter the alarming flow of English into French, France's language gendarmes insist that what Americanism be displaced by *prêt-à-manger*?

GAME 15—LEVEL VI

26. WORD EVOLUTIONS What word came from a Greek word that means *to be inspired*, appeared in English in 1603 defined as *belief in special revelations of the Holy Spirit*, was later defined as *religious fanaticism*, and is now used to mean *ardent zeal for a cause or subject*?

27. EPONYMS What is the family name of British land agent

Charles C. ___, who, while assigned to Ireland's County Mayo in 1880, was rendered ineffective when a large segment of the population blackballed him for his refusal to reduce property rents?

28. **GENERAL QUESTIONS** In 1936, what name was coined for *language that appears to be meaningful but which, in fact, is a mixture of sense and nonsense,* such as: *"For a new word to prove kersome, it must be plushtive and have resonating ominence marked by a distinct grammancy with overtones of subtly connected furshion"?*

29. **BRITICISMS** In Britain, what is a *geyser?*
    a. a water heater
    b. a powerful air fan
    c. a peculiar or weird person

30. **WORD EVOLUTIONS** When Samuel Johnson published his dictionary in the mid-eighteenth century, the letter *J* was still called the consonant form of the letter *I.* In what order, therefore, did these words appear in his dictionary: *JILT, ILEUS, IGNORE?*

ANSWERS

GAME 15

GAME 15—Level I—1 Point Each

1. fin—which appeared in English in 1925
2. c—unnecessarily complex contraptions
3. stink bomb
4. potato
5. mud, as in *mud slinger*

GAME 15—Level II—2 Points Each

6. acoustic
7. one cubit
8. necklace / neckless
9. "What's up?"
10. parfait

GAME 15—Level III—3 Points Each

11. *m-o-t-o-c-r-o-s-s*
12. wisenheimer—which is a blend of *wise* and *-enheimer*, as was found in such illustrious names of the time as Opp*enheimer*, Gugg*enheimer*, and others
13. c—micromanager
14. cum laude—which also translates to *with distinction*
15. c—England, in the 13th century

GAME 15—Level IV—4 Points Each

16. jodhpur—from *Jodhpur*, India
17. a—double-barreled
18. nickel—from the German *Nickel*, which means *goblin* and was the name chosen by the Germans as a result of the deceptive reddish copper color of the mineral niccolite, which is a nickel arsenide
19. the ampersand (&)—from Latin *et* (and)
20. a—nothing, the historical record demonstrates that such pronouncements, if noticed, are blissfully and routinely ignored

GAME 15—Level V—5 Points Each

21. 1789—De la Platière became minister of France after the French Revolution and had earlier predicted that *American* English would one day replace French as the world language, much to the consternation of some French *and* British.
22. Richard Nixon—who used the term for those who did not join the highly vocal forces of dissent against the war in Vietnam and, he assumed, agreed with his position
23. Miss Piggy
24. c—H.L. Mencken, in *The American Language* (1919)
25. fast food

GAME 15—Level VI—6 Points Each

26. enthusiasm
27. Boycott
28. double-talk
29. a—a water heater
30. IGNORE, JILT, ILEUS

BETHUMP'D REGULAR
GAME 16

GAME 16—LEVEL I

1. **WORD EVOLUTIONS** What word was derived from the word *move* as soon as there was need for a name for *a succession of pictures that produces an optical effect of motion*?

2. **EPONYMS** What radioactive element is named after the planet *Uranus*?

3. **LETTER WORDS** What do economists mean when they use the letter word *GNP*?

4. **IDIOMS** Idiomatically speaking, what is meant by the statement *"They're not too swift"*?
   a. they're swift enough
   b. they do things slowly
   c. they're not very intelligent

5. **SLANG** On U.S. college campuses, is a *fake bake* a cake made with ingredients containing artificial additives, a tanning salon session, or a sweat-provoking quiz that doesn't count toward one's grade?

GAME 16—LEVEL II

6. **AMERICANISMS** In 1943, what slang-type term for *a wall hanging* was firmly implanted in the English language with

the curvaceous help of Betty Grable?

7. **NAMES / NICKNAMES** In 1931, what name was coined for *the underground trading of goods in violation of official regulations*?

8. **TRUE OR FALSE** The first American-born generation of nearly every group of immigrants spoke or speaks English with the accents of their parents' language.

9. **ACRONYMS** What organization of Native Americans is known by the acronym *AIM*?

10. **HOMOPHONES** Identify and spell the homophones defined as:
   a. a racing shell rowed by one or more persons
   b. the skeleton of the head

GAME 16—LEVEL III

11. **GENERAL QUESTIONS** Which of these groups of word-smiths is more likely to become unglued by English's seeming endless list of irregularities?
   a. lexicographers
   b. philologists
   c. grammarians

12. **EPONYMS** During the late 19th century, what *tart green fruit* was cultivated near Sydney, Australia by Maria Ann Smith?

13. **NAMES / NICKNAMES** What Manhattan, New York restaurant contributed the names *Baked Alaska*, *Lobster Newburg*, and *Delmonico Steak* to English's culinary lingo?

14. **GLOBAL ENGLISH** As indicated by borrowed words and usages, which of these versions of English do German lin-

guists say has had the greatest impact on late 20th German: American, Australian, British, or Canadian?

15. BORROWED WORDS Though English originated as a Germanic language, is its clearly evident Romance language character mostly due to its aggressive borrowing of words from Spanish, French, or Italian?

GAME 16—LEVEL IV

16. EPONYMS Sometime around 1933, which of these words was derived from the name of French statesman Comte François N. Mollien?
  a. moll
  b. molly
  c. mollify

17. WORD EVOLUTIONS In what order did the words *teener*, *teenager*, and *teens* appear in English?

18. PORTMANTEAU WORDS What words did Richard Corliss blend when he wrote: "By now (Sylvester) Stallone has become a symbol for all that is goofy and grandiloquent in Hollywood's live-action summer cartoons. The hormone that courses through his movie veins could be called *preposterone*"?

19. BORROWED WORDS In 1544, *comrade* appeared in English as a derivative of the Middle French word that is spelled *c-a-m-a-r-a-d-e* and has what literal meaning?
  a. roommate
  b. camel parade
  c. communist

20. BRITICISMS In Britain, is *badmash* sour chicken feed, stolen or illicit money, or a hooligan?

21. AUSTRALIANISMS In Australia, which of the following is known as a *rort*?
    a. a wild and noisy party
    b. a runt pig
    c. a painfully silenced belch

22. EPONYMS Which of these physical phenomena was demonstrated by Scottish botanist and naturalist Robert Brown (1773-1858)?
    a. electricity power drops
    b. the vibratory actions of microscopic particles
    c. oxidation reactions in fruit

23. ACRONYMS What do accountants mean when they use the acronym *FIFO*?

24. IDIOMS What competitive dance invented by African-Americans parodied white dancing, awarded winners with a cake, usually coconut, and gave rise to idiomatic statements such as *That takes the cake* and *That's a piece of cake*?

25. HOMOPHONES Identify and spell the homophones defined as:
    a. the trigonometric function that, for an acute angle, is the ratio between the leg adjacent to the angle, when it is considered part of a right triangle, and the hypotenuse
    b. to sign jointly

GAME 16—LEVEL VI

26. HISTORY What annals were the first ever to be published in English, beginning around 891 in the court of Alfred the Great and continuing on in monasteries until 1154?

27. IDIOMS The word *pale* in the idiomatic expression *beyond* *the pale*, which means *something that is disgraceful or unacceptable*, came from which of these concepts?

    a. an appalling act that inspires disgust
    b. to cause a pale or pallid complexion
    c. on the other side of the palisade

28. WORD ORIGINS In India in 1786, in what lone ancient language did British judge William Jones discover the ancestral roots of Latin, French, Spanish, Russian, Celtic, Gaelic, German, Dutch, and English?

29. GLOBAL ENGLISH In an attempt to thwart the linguistic imperialism of *"la langue du Coca-Cola,"* what Americanism did the French lingo guards insist be translated as *capitaux fébriles*?

30. ACRONYMS What is meant by the acronym *NASDAQ*?

ANSWERS
GAME 16

GAME 16—Level I—1 Point Each

1. movie—which appeared in 1912
2. uranium
3. *Gross National Product*—which is *the total value of the goods and services produced by a nation during a given period of time*
4. c—they're not very intelligent
5. a tanning salon session

GAME 16—Level II—2 Points Each

6. pin-up
7. black market
8. False—most spoke or speak English with the accents of their American peer group
9. *American Indian Movement*
10. *s-c-u-l-l* / *s-k-u-l-l*

GAME 16—Level III—3 Points Each

11. c—grammarians, who are often accused of attempting to impose lifeless regularity on the language
12. apples—which in 1895 became known as *Granny Smith* apples
13. Delmonico's—which was founded by Lorenzo Delmonico in the 19th century

14. American—which began to displace the British English influence soon after WWII
15. French

GAME 16—Level IV—4 Points Each

16. b—molly, the aquarium fish
17. teens (1604), teener (1894), teenager (1939)
18. *preposterous* + *testosterone*
19. a—roommate
20. a hooligan

GAME 16—Level V—5 Points Each

21. a—a wild and noisy party. Australians also use the word to mean *a fraud or racket.*
22. b—the vibratory actions of microscopic particles, which is now known as *brownian movement or motion*
23. *F*irst *I*n, *F*irst *O*ut—a term applied to the practice of always using the oldest portion of inventory first
24. The Cakewalk—which appeared in English in 1879 and also in the 1940 film *Stormy Weather* starring Lena Horne and Bill Robinson
25. cosine / co-sign

GAME 16—Level VI—6 Points Each

26. *Anglo-Saxon Chronicles*
27. c—on the other side of the *palisade*, a fence of stakes set up for defensive purposes
28. Sanskrit
29. hot money
30. *N*ational *A*ssociation of *S*ecurities *D*ealers *A*utomated *Q*uotations

BETHUMP'D REGULAR
GAME 17

GAME 17—LEVEL I

1. **NAMES / NICKNAMES** Are *mushers* a winery's crew of purple-legged grape stompers, overly passionate lovers, or people who travel by dog sled?

2. **EPONYMS** What type of puzzle got its name from that of *a thin-bladed saw that is capable of cutting fine lines*?

3. **HISTORY** In what order did the names of these colors appear in English: *purple*, *mauve*, *red*?

4. **IDIOMS** Idiomatically speaking, does a *yellow dog* have a disposition that is sweet, mellow, or mean?

5. **SLANG** In 1889, what term was coined by soldiers for use as a name for their *civilian clothes*?

GAME 17—LEVEL II

6. **EPONYMS** What award, given annually since 1946 for out-standing achievement in the theater, was named in honor of American actor and producer Antoinette Perry?

7. **NAMES / NICKNAMES** What *nickname for the U.S. flag* was coined on March 17, 1824 by William Driver of Salem, Massachusetts, the 21-year-old captain of the merchant ship

Charles Doggett?

8. **BORROWED WORDS** In about 1718, what name for a floral arrangement came into English from the Old French word that is spelled *b-o-s-q-u-e-t* and has the literal meaning of *little forest* or *a thicket*?

9. **LINGUISTICS** In the jargon of linguistics, which of the following are examples of *reduplicatives* that are in common use in mainstream English?
   a. poor, poorer, poorest
   b. good, great, magnificent
   c. goody-goody, so-so, tom-tom

10. **SLANG** In 1832, what redundant and hyphenated term appeared in English defined as *a strong virile man*?

GAME 17—LEVEL III

11. **JARGON** In the jargon of the theater, what is meant by the letter word *O.B.*, which also appears with the spelling *o-b-i-e*?
   a. *Off Beat*
   b. *Off Broadway*
   c. *OBit* (for critiques of performances that bomb)

12. **HOMOPHONES** A grizzly walking around with a case of alopecia that runs from stem to stern can be called a ___ ___.

13. **WORD EVOLUTIONS** What word evolved out of the Middle English word that is spelled *g-o-g-e-l-e-n* and means *to squint*?

14. **AMERICANISMS** Which of the following triplets was coined in America?
   a. lengthy, immigrant, seaboard
   b. ski, skin, sky
   c. beef, pork, champagne

15. NAMES / NICKNAMES In 1997, what U.S. president had an orange-yellow rose named in his honor by The Netherlands, in part, because of his Dutch ancestry and family name, which means *rose field* in Dutch?

GAME 17—LEVEL IV

16. WORD ORIGINS What word originated in the Old Italian word that is spelled *b-r-a-v-a-r-e* and means *to challenge, show off* and is now used to mean *blustering swaggering conduct* and *a pretense of bravery*?

17. CANADIANISMS Which of these nicknames did Canadians coin for their weakening dollars during the worldwide financial crises of the late 1990s?
    a. Dizzy Lizzies
    b. Northern Lites
    c. Limp Loonies

18. NAMES / NICKNAMES In 1848, what name coined in 1809 by Washington Irving was used for the first time as *a generic nickname for denizens of New York City*?

19. BRITICISMS In Britain, who or what is affectionately called *Aunty Beeb*?
    a. Queen Elizabeth
    b. the BBC
    c. the wife of John Bull, British cousin of Uncle Sam

20. AUSTRALIANISMS In Australia, is a *tinnie* a can of beer, an English Ford, or a metal roof?

GAME 17—LEVEL V

21. QUOTATIONS On January 24, 1771, what word did Voltaire use when he wrote: *"The first among ___ is that which possesses the largest number of excellent works"*?

a. libraries
b. nations
c. languages

22. **WORD EVOLUTIONS** Which of the early lexicographers of English underscored the ever-evolving nature of language when he wrote: *"... may the lexicographer be derided who, being able to produce no example of a nation that has preserved their words and phrases from mutability, shall (imagine) that his dictionary can embalm his language... "*?

23. **BRITICISMS** In Britain, what is meant if a person says, "*I think I might go spare*"?
    a. they might go crazy or become angry
    b. they might borrow something from a neighbor
    c. they might join a couple as the third party on a date

24. **PIDGINS & CREOLES** Which of these languages is defined as *an English-based creole, with a vocabulary and grammatical elements from various African languages, that is spoken by African-Americans on the islands and coastal region of southeastern United States*?
    a. Tok Pisin
    b. Ebonics
    c. Gullah

25. **BORROWED WORDS** In 1806, the culinary term *au gratin* was borrowed from French where it has which of these literal meanings?
    a. with grating
    b. with gracious helpings
    c. with burnt scrapings from the pan

GAME 17—LEVEL VI

26. **HISTORY** In 1530, was the first grammar of French, *Lesclarcissement de la Langue Françoyse*, written by a citizen

of France, Belgium, or Britain?

27. NAMES / NICKNAMES In March 1998, what false alarm that embarrassed and infuriated NASA officials was dubbed *"the Chicken Little furor"*?

28. BRITICISMS Amidst the many regional dialects of Britain, what animal is known variously as a *cuddy*, *moke*, *nirrup*, and *pronkus*?
    a. donkey
    b. rabbit
    c. polled Hereford steer

29. BORROWED WORDS The *coco* of *coco*nut came into English via Spanish and Portuguese where it has which of the following meanings?
    a. crazy
    b. Caucasian
    c. bogeyman

30. HISTORY During WWII in the Pacific, after repeated failures by experienced cryptographers to develop an unbreakable code, what small group of wholly inexperienced American soldiers was credited with inventing, in effect, a double-coded system of communication involving the Roman alphabet that proved impossible for the Japanese to decipher?

ANSWERS

GAME 17

GAME 17—Level I—1 Point Each

1. people who travel by dog sled
2. jigsaw
3. red (before the 12th century); purple (15th century); mauve (1859)
4. mean
5. civies

GAME 17—Level II—2 Points Each

6. the Tony
7. Old Glory
8. bouquet
9. c—goody-goody, so-so, tom-tom
10. he-man—It is interesting that *Heman* was a relatively common first name for boys before the advent of this term and all but disappeared afterward.

GAME 17—Level III—3 Points Each

11. b—*Off* Broadway
12. bare / bear
13. goggle—which gave rise to *goggle-eyed*, *goggles*, and so on
14. a—lengthy, immigrant, seaboard
15. Franklin Delano Roosevelt—who was a descendant of 1648 Dutch immigrant to the New World, Claes van *Rosenvelt*

GAME 17—Level IV—4 Points Each

16. bravado
17. Limp Loonies—the Canadian dollar coin features a *loon*
18. knickerbocker—which came from Diedrich *Knickerbocker*, Irving's fictitious author of *History of New York*
19. b—the BBC
20. a can of beer

GAME 17—Level V—5 Points Each

21. c—languages
22. Samuel Johnson (1755)
23. a—they might go crazy or become angry
24. c—Gullah
25. c—with burnt scrapings from the pan

GAME 17—Level VI—6 Points Each

26. Britain—by Englishman John Palsgrave
27. the too hasty and, thankfully, erroneous announcement by astronomers that a mile-wide asteroid was on a collision course with the Earth
28. a—donkey
29. bogeyman—because the nut resembles a grotesque human face
30. Navajos—who, basing the code on their native language, became known as the *Navajo Code Talkers*

BETHUMP'D REGULAR
GAME 18

GAME 18—LEVEL I

1. **ACRONYMS** What department of the U.S. government is known by the acronym *HUD*?

2. **IDIOMS** Idiomatically speaking, is a person who is *a ball of fire* unusually energetic, a pyromaniac, or a circus' inept flame eater?

3. **WORD ORIGINS** What word that appeared in English in the 14th century is of Celtic origin and is akin to the Middle Irish word for *bell*, which is spelled *c-l-o-c-c*?

4. **EPONYMS** Which of these words did Lewis Carroll coin for use as the title of a nonsense poem?
   a. jabberwocky
   b. gibberish
   c. blather

5. **ACCENTS** Do London's Cockneys say *itch* when they mean stitch, pitch, or hitch?

GAME 18—LEVEL II

6. **SLANG** In the street lingo of the 1990s, what problem is suffered by the guy who is said to be *sugar-free*?
   a. hypoglycemia

b. artificial sweetness, i.e., he's a phoney

c. GDS or *Girlfriend Deficiency Syndrome*

7. **BRITICISMS** If a native of Britain says, *"Sir Percival eats Yank-way,"* does Percy hold his knife, fork, or spoon with his right hand?

8. **NAMES / NICKNAMES** In about 1960, what word was coined as the name for *the highly jargonized language used by computer technologists*?

9. **BORROWED WORDS** In 1886, what name for *a loose dressing gown with wide sleeves* was borrowed from Japanese where it has the not-too-descriptive meaning of *wearing thing*?

10. **PORTMANTEAU WORDS** In 1973, what name appeared in English defined as *a hybrid animal that is 5/8 domestic meat-type bovine and 3/8 North American bison*?

GAME 18—LEVEL III

11. **WORD ORIGINS** In 1938, what name for *a vigorous acrobatic dance* was coined by combining a word that means *to act nervously* with *the common name for a crawling or creeping invertebrate*?

12. **IDIOMS** In the jargon of clothing designers, is a style that is said to be *off the boat* a startling new product of European designers, frumpish, or one that is popular with sailors?

13. **SLANG** What slang term for *nose* is akin to the German word that means *snout*, which is spelled *S-c-h-n-a-u-z-e*, and was used over and again in the humor of Jimmy Durante?

14. **WORD ORIGINS** What name for *a standard unit of distance that is used primarily in horse racing* evolved out of the

Old English concept of *the ideal length of the longest furrow to be plowed when plowing a field*?

15. **HISTORY** In 1996, France was infuriated by the U.S. veto of Boutros Boutros-Ghali's re-election to Secretary-General of the United Nations and demanded the next Secretary-General be which of the following?
   a. French
   b. chosen by France
   c. fluent in French

GAME 18—LEVEL IV

16. **HISTORY** Did H.L. Mencken believe immigrants and their native languages were a threat, an asset, or of little consequence to American English?

17. **PIDGINS & CREOLES** When a form of pidgin English evolves into a more consistent and complex form it loses its pidgin classification and becomes known as which of the following?
   a. a dialect
   b. a creole
   c. a patois

18. **DINOSAUR WORDS** What does one haul into the house if a person says, *"I'd like you to bring in the sheaves"*?
   a. house shingles
   b. bound stalks of grain
   c. the female sheep

19. **JARGON** In the jargon of the military, between 1922 and 1944 what happened to soldiers who were inept or had bad traits and were given *Section Eights*?
   a. they were discharged
   b. they were put in solitary confinement
   c. they were committed to mental institutes

20. IDIOMS Which of the following is *the place where one envisions oneself to be when an atomic bomb is dropped,* according to D. Coupland's 1991 novel *Generation X*?
   a. Wrongs-ville
   b. Out of Place
   c. mental ground zero

GAME 18—LEVEL V

21. HISTORY Which of these universities was the first to establish a press for the publication of scholarly works written in American English?
   a. Harvard
   b. Princeton
   c. Cornell

22. ACCENTS In 1913, which of these groups did Britain's Robert Bridges, founder of The Society for Pure English, see as a language imperiling menace due to what he called its *"blundering corruptions and mutilations"* of English?
   a. London's Cockneys
   b. Australians
   c. America's immigrants

23. WORD EVOLUTIONS In 1755, was Samuel Johnson referring the letter x, y, or z when he wrote: *"(It) is a letter which, though found* (within) *Saxon words, begins no word in the English language"*?

24. GLOBAL ENGLISH In the 1980s, why was it said that *"The face of Kathy Flower is better recognized in China than that of Queen Elizabeth"*?
   a. though British, she spoke fluent Mandarin
   b. she moderated the BBC's English language learning series *Follow Me*
   c. she translated the King James Bible into Chinese

25. BORROWED WORDS In the 13th century, what word that is now defined as *suave, urbane* was borrowed from French where it is literally defined as *of good family or nature?*

GAME 18—LEVEL VI

26. HOMOPHONES Identify and spell the homophones that complete this sentence: *A colorful and coquettish carp that is bred in Japan for stocking ornamental ponds is a ___ ___.*

27. HISTORY In 1957-58, what was the goal of the public competition that was financed by a bequest from the estate of George Bernard Shaw?
    a. identify the person who coined *boogie-woogie*
    b. coin ten words based on unused Latin terms
    c. design an alphabet with at least 40 letters

28. LINGUISTICS Which of the following characterizes those who suffer *pleonasm?*
    a. they stutter
    b. they use *too few* words to adequately convey their thoughts
    c. they use *more* words than necessary to convey their thoughts

29. WORD EVOLUTIONS What colloquial-type word that came from French was originally used to mean *later born*, is now used as a legal term that is spelled *p-u-i-s-n-e* and means *younger or inferior in rank*, and, in ordinary language, has an anglicized spelling and is defined as *weak or inferior?*

30. EPONYMS What is the family name of artilleryman Henry ___ who, in 1803, invented an antipersonnel weapon comprising a hollow spherical projectile filled with shot and an explosive charge, which was quickly adopted by the British military?

ANSWERS

GAME 18

GAME 18—Level I—1 Point Each

1. *H*ousing and *U*rban *D*evelopment
2. unusually energetic
3. clock
4. a—jabberwocky, which has since become an eponym defined as *meaningless speech or writing*
5. hitch

GAME 18—Level II—2 Points Each

6. c—GDS or *G*irlfriend *D*eficiency *S*yndrome, that is, he lacks a girlfriend
7. fork—in contrast, the British are schooled to hold the knife with their right hand
8. computerese
9. kimono—from *ki* (wearing) + *mono* (thing)
10. beefalo

GAME 18—Level III—3 Points Each

11. jitterbug
12. frumpish—the term is an allusion to the clothing worn by newly arriving, usually poor, immigrants
13. *schnozz* or *schnozzal* or even *schnozzola*—each of which is more directly rooted in Yiddish's *shnoitsl*
14. furlong—which is equal to 220 yards, about the distance a team of horses or oxen can pull a plow before it needs a

moment's rest
15. c—fluent in French

GAME 18—Level IV—4 Points Each

16. an asset—that, according to Mencken, presents opportunities to infuse the language with new words that will enhance its hybrid vigor
17. b—a creole
18. b—bound stalks of grain
19. a—they were discharged, based on the provisions of *Section VIII, Army Regulation 615-360*
20. c—mental ground zero

GAME 18—Level V—5 Points Each

21. Cornell—in 1869, which was followed by Johns Hopkins University in 1878 and the University of Chicago in 1891
22. c—America's immigrants
23. x
24. b—she moderated the BBC's English language learning series, *Follow Me*, which estimates indicate had an audience that ranged from 50-million to more than the population of the United States
25. debonair—which came from the Old French *de bon aire*

GAME 18—Level VI—6 Points Each

26. *c-o-y / k-o-i*
27. c—design an alphabet with at least 40 letters
28. c—they use *more* words than necessary to convey their thoughts
29. puny
30. Shrapnel

BETHUMP'D REGULAR
GAME 19

GAME 19—LEVEL I

1. **HISTORY** When it was first minted in 1792, what U.S. coin was imprinted with the French word that is spelled *d-i-s-m-e*?

2. **GENERAL QUESTIONS** As a group, are the words *gaudy*, *garish*, and *tacky* eponyms, antonyms, or synonyms?

3. **BORROWED WORDS** What name for *blue denim* evolved from the Hindi name for *a coarse calico*, which is phonetically spelled *d-u-g-r-i*?

4. **AMERICANISMS** In about 1960, what term did American college students coin for *an unexpected quickie test*?

5. **BRITICISMS** In Britain, is a person who is said to have *a face like the back of a bus* expressionless, ugly, or pale and exhausted?

GAME 19—LEVEL II

6. **NAMES / NICKNAMES** In 1646, what word was coined as a shortened and altered form of the word *university*, is still used in Britain to mean *university*, but in the United States is defined as *the principal squad representing a school in a sport*?

7. **IDIOMS** What term that is derived from the name of a card game is defined as *the facial expression of a person who has the ability to hide her/his thoughts*?

8. **WORD EVOLUTIONS** In the 14th century, what words did Geoffrey Chaucer spell *n-o-m-b-r-e-s*, *f-r-a-c-c-i-o-n-s*, and *c-o-n-s-e-n-t-r-i-k-e*?

9. **JARGON** In the culinary lingo of hunters, what meat is known as *high speed beef*?

10. **SLANG** In 1996, what term appeared in the *Random House Compact Unabridged Dictionary* defined as *an unstimulating, low-wage job with few benefits*?
    a. McJob
    b. entry-job
    c. serf-job

GAME 19—LEVEL III

11. **PORTMANTEAU WORDS** In the 1990s, what professional golfer blended the words Caucasian, Black, Indian, and Asian to form the word *Cablinasian*?

12. **NAMES / NICKNAMES** Which of these computer gurus invented the name *World Wide Web* and recommended use of the letter word *www*?
    a. Bill Gates, at Microsoft
    b. Tim Berners-Lee, at CERN
    c. Steve Jobs, at Apple

13. **PIDGINS & CREOLES** In Cameroon Creole, what is a designing young man planning to do to his mother if he says he's going into the house to *swit mot* (sweet mouth) her?
    a. kiss her
    b. flatter her
    c. ask her to use a breath freshener

14. BORROWED WORDS Because the loudness of the string-plucked harpsichord was not controllable, Bartolommeo Cristofori of Florence invented what instrument with sound control that is now known by an Italian word that means *soft*?

15. EPONYMS During the 17th century, a sleek two-masted ship was often used for the temporary offshore confinement of wayward sailors, a practice that led to the use of what colloquial term for *prison*?

GAME 19—LEVEL IV

16. WORD EVOLUTIONS In 1688, what word was defined as a *woman's ornate cap*, was later defined as *a low chest of drawers*, and today is defined as *a toilet*?

17. EPONYMS In 1889, which of these words came into English from the name of a game invented by British comedian Arthur Roberts?
   a. spoof
   b. spook
   c. spoon

18. HOMOPHONES Identify and spell the homophones defined as:
   a. to send forth by throwing
   b. a system of rigid social stratification based on wealth, inherited rank, privilege, and other factors

19. HOMOGRAPHS Spell the homographs that are defined as *the cast-off skin of a snake* and *a place of deep mud* and which, respectively, are alternately and increasingly spelled *s-l-u-f-f* and *s-l-u-e*.

20. BORROWED WORDS What word is defined as *a long parley, idle talk, or misleading speech* and came from the Portuguese word that means *word* and is spelled *p-a-l-a-v-r-a*?

GAME 19—LEVEL V

21. GLOBAL ENGLISH During the early days of India's independence from Britain, who triumphantly but erroneously predicted that within one generation English would no longer be used in India?
   a. Mahatma Gandhi
   b. Charles de Gaulle
   c. Jawaharlal Nehru

22. HOMOPHONES Identify and spell the homophones defined as:
   a. the sense of taste
   b. a wooden flat-bladed instrument

23. BRITICISMS In 1936, before Britain's Advisory Committee on Spoken English settled on *roundabouts* as a name for *traffic circles*, which of the following was given serious consideration?
   a. collector circles
   b. gyratory circuses
   c. shuttle rings

24. HISTORY If English is now used by 750-million to as many a one-billion people, about how many used it during the time of William Shakespeare, the late 16th to early 17th centuries?
   a. 5-7 million
   b. 25-28 million
   c. 50-70 million

25. PORTMANTEAU WORDS What portmanteau term did author Alex Haley use when he described his book *Roots* as *part fiction, part fact*?

GAME 19—LEVEL VI

26. WORD EVOLUTIONS What name for a metal tool

evolved into a synonym for *cheater* because it was used by dishonest money handlers to shave or chip off pieces from coins for use in minting more coins?

27. ACRONYMS In computerese, what is meant by *ASCII*?

28. BORROWED WORDS The Old English word that is spelled *w-l-i-t-e* and defined as *countenance* was displaced during the 13th century with what word from French?

29. BRITICISMS In Britain, what characteristic does a thing have if a native says, *"It's bloody codswallop"*?
   a. it reeks like rotten cod
   b. it's complete nonsense
   c. it's beaten beyond recognition

30. EPONYMS In 1845, what element was identified as a component of the rare mineral tantalite, which was named after Lydian king Tantalus, and was, therefore, named after King Tantalus' daughter *Niobe*?

ANSWERS
GAME 19

GAME 19—Level I—1 Point Each

1. dime
2. synonyms
3. dungaree—which appeared in English in 1573
4. pop quiz
5. ugly

GAME 19—Level II—2 Points Each

6. varsity
7. poker-faced
8. numbers, fractions, concentric
9. venison
10. a—McJob

GAME 19—Level III—3 Points Each

11. Tiger Woods—who used it as an abbreviated response for those who inquired about his racial heritage
12. b—Tim Berners-Lee, at CERN
13. b—flatter her
14. piano—which appeared in English in 1803
15. brig—from *brigantine*

GAME 19—Level IV—4 Points Each

16. commode

17. a—spoof, from Roberts' hoaxing game *Spoof*
18. *c-a-s-t* / *c-a-s-t-e*
19. *s-l-o-u-g-h* / *s-l-o-u-g-h*
20. palaver

GAME 19—Level V—5 Points Each

21. Jawaharlal Nehru—India's first prime minister
22. *p-a-l-a-t-e* / *p-a-l-l-e-t*
23. b—gyratory circuses
24. a—5-7 million
25. faction

GAME 19—Level VI—6 Points Each

26. chisel—from which came *chiseler*
27. *A*merican *S*tandard *C*ode for *I*nformation *I*nterchange
28. face
29. b—it's complete nonsense
30. niobium

BETHUMP'D REGULAR
GAME 20

GAME 20—LEVEL I

1. **NAMES / NICKNAMES** Which of these fruit is the only to have the same name from the time it is picked until the time it is eaten: *raisin, orange, prune*?

2. **WORD ORIGINS** What word evolved out of a 15th century spelling mistake that involved the leftward shifting of the first *n* in the term *a napron*?

3. **PIDGINS & CREOLES** In 1834, which of these reduplicatives that mean *do it quickly* was borrowed into mainstream English from Chinese pidgin English?
   - a. go-go
   - b. come-come
   - c. chop-chop

4. **WORD EVOLUTIONS** In about 1500, what word was defined as *a helpful good-natured elf*, was later used to mean *a first grade Girl Scout* and, a bit later, *a small square of rich chocolate cake*?

5. **EPONYMS** In 1876, what name was given to the *cathartic hydrated magnesium sulfate that was produced from the water flowing out of a mineral spring in Epsom, England*?

GAME 20—LEVEL II

6. **BRITICISMS** While most speakers of American English use *learned* as the past tense of *to learn*, what is used by most speakers of British English?

7. **PORTMANTEAU WORDS** In 1942, what material that is used in incendiary bombs was named by blending the words *palmitate* and *naphthene*?

8. **WORD EVOLUTIONS** In 1725, which of these words appeared in English defined as *infested with maggots*?
    a. grubby
    b. filthy
    c. dirty

9. **NAMES / NICKNAMES** What nickname is used for the *Federal National Mortgage Association*?

10. **WORD ORIGINS** What title for a member of a medical profession appeared in English in 1646 as a derivative of a Latin word that means *of beasts of burden*?

GAME 20—LEVEL III

11. **CANADIANISMS** In Canada, what is known as *a Hollywood stop*?
    a. ignoring and driving through a stop sign
    b. an overly theatrical conclusion to an argument
    c. a visit to the theater

12. **ACCENTS** In which of these countries is English spoken with the *least* amount of uniformity?
    a. United States, with about 3.5 million square miles
    b. Australia, with about 3 million square miles
    c. Britain, with about 50,000 square miles

13. **SLANG** Sometime around 1891, which of these terms appeared in English defined as *soldiers who are considered expendable in battle*: Kilroys, cannon fodder, or sitting ducks?

14. **EPONYMS** What is the family name of the George M. ___ who, in the 19th century, built the first luxurious railroad passenger car?

15. **HOMOPHONES** Identify and spell the homophones defined as:
    a. a variety of rock dove
    b. a simplified form of speech used for communication between people who speak different languages

GAME 20—LEVEL IV

16. **WORD ORIGINS** What word appeared in English in 1676 as a result of the high speed British pronunciation of the name *Saint Audrey*?

17. **ACRONYMS** During congressional debates about extending the draft prior to WWII, what was meant by the acronym *OHIO* that began to appear as graffiti on the walls of the nation's frustrated military camps?
    a. *O*h *H*ell, *I*'m (an) *O*bit
    b. *O*ver (the) *H*ill *I*n *O*ctober
    c. *O*kay *H*itler, *I*t's *O*ver

18. **BRITICISMS** In Britain, what are *God spots*?
    a. fruit blemishes
    b. televised religious programs
    c. the anomalous spots seen after looking heavenward, especially at the sun

19. **SLANG** What is a *simoleon*, a term that appeared in English in 1896 from an unknown source?
    a. a dollar

b. an example of behavior similar to Napoleon's

c. a cheap, usually fake floor covering

20. WORD EVOLUTIONS   What word started out defined as *a mercenary soldier, especially of the Middle Ages*, and is now defined as *a person who works without a long-term commitment to any one employer*?

GAME 20—LEVEL V

21. EPONYMS   Name the fair that was held near Dublin, Ireland every year for some 651 years and gained legendary notoriety as a result of the traditional consumption of enormous quantities of liquor and the inevitable and gleeful eruption of free-for-all brawling.

22. WORD EVOLUTIONS   In 1362, what word was coined by William Langland and defined as *eggs that are small and misshapen, as if laid by a cock;* was used by Chaucer to mean *a milksop or mother's darling;* was used to mean *city slicker* in the 16th century; and, now, is defined as *a working class Londoner, especially one from the East End*?

23. BRITICISMS   In Britain, what actually happened if someone says: *"After losing the match, the entire rugger team went into a wax"*?

a. the team screamed and wailed in unified hysteria

b. the team got pathologically depressed

c. the team went raving mad

24. WORD ORIGINS   What large fish-eating bird got its name from the Latin word *ossifraga*, which means *bone breaker*, even though the bird gulps its food and shows no inclination whatsoever toward busting bones?

25. NAMES / NICKNAMES   What common name for the black-footed albatross is also used to mean *simpleton*?

26. GLOBAL ENGLISH What happened in the ten years following 1899 when Hermann Dunger published a treatise entitled *Against the Englishisms in the German Language*?
   a. nothing
   b. a wave of anglophobia swept the country
   c. Englishisms in German grew by more than 400%

27. ACCENTS In Britain, what was said about the accent of Northumbrian Wilfred Pickles after he began to read the BBC's news during WWII?
   a. it compromised the integrity of the news
   b. it was so perfect it was cold and inhuman
   c. it was pathetically comical yet entertaining

28. PIDGINS & CREOLES In 1711, what word appeared in mainstream English as a phonetic rendition of the Chinese Pidgin English pronunciation of the Portuguese word for *god*, which is spelled *d-e-u-s*?

29. BORROWED WORDS In 1697, what word was borrowed intact from French where it has the literal meaning of *head-to-head*, and is now used primarily to mean *a private conversation between two people*?

30. NAMES / NICKNAMES What is the family name of André ___, France's minister of war, who, at a January 1930 vote in the Chamber of Deputies, was the main speaker supporting the construction of an anti-German frontier fortress?

ANSWERS

GAME 20

GAME 20—Level I—1 Point Each

1. orange—a raisin was once a grape; a prune was once a plum
2. apron—which, with the *n*-shift, became *an apron*
3. c—chop-chop
4. brownie
5. Epsom salts

GAME 20—Level II—2 Points Each

6. learnt
7. napalm
8. a—grubby
9. Fannie Mae
10. veterinarian—from the Latin *veterinarius*

GAME 20—Level III—3 Points Each

11. a—ignoring and driving through a stop sign
12. c—Britain, with about 50,000 square miles
13. cannon fodder
14. Pullman—which, in 1867, was also used as the name for the car
15. *p-i-g-e-o-n / p-i-d-g-i-n*

GAME 20—Level IV—4 Points Each

16. tawdry

17. b—*Over* (the) *Hill In October*, a surreptitiously planned mass desertion. The attitude, however, was quickly reversed when the Japanese bombed Pearl Harbor.
18. b—televised religious programs
19. a—a dollar
20. freelancer

GAME 20—Level V—5 Points Each

21. Donnybrook
22. Cockney—from *cockeneye* in Langland's *Piers Plowman*
23. c—the team went raving mad
24. osprey
25. gooney

GAME 20—Level VI—6 Points Each

26. c—Englishisms in German grew by more than 400%
27. a—it compromised the integrity of the news
28. joss—which is now defined as *a Chinese idol or cult image*
29. tête-à-tête
30. Maginot

SECTION III

BETHUMP'D LITE

HIGH NUTRIENT
WORD SNACKS
FOR
LOW FAT MOMENTS

Answers are at the end of the section, starting on page 255

BETHUMP'D LITE
GAME 1

Level I (one point each)

1. **HOMONYMS** Identify the homonyms in this sentence: *The boss had to ___ the klutz who started a ___ in a wastebasket.*

2. **IDIOMS** What animal is *let out of the bag* when you pass on a secret you were supposed to keep to yourself?

3. **NAMES / NICKNAMES** What large East Coast U.S. city is nicknamed *The Big Apple*?

Level II (two points each)

4. **WORD ORIGINS** In 1964, what 34-letter word was made famous by Mary Poppins?

5. **HOMOPHONES** Two-thirds of the donuts were gone, leaving four, so we know the boys ___ ___ of them.

6. **LETTER WORDS** What phrase means *do it quickly* and is abbreviated with the letters *ASAP*?

Level III (three points each)

7. **PORTMANTEAU WORDS** In 1913, what word was created by blending the words *motor* and *cavalcade*?

8. **BORROWED WORDS** What state's name came from the Chippewa Indian words *mici*, which means *big*, and *sibi*, which means *river*?

9. **AMERICANISMS** What American-born slang term means *to scorn or show disrespect to*?

Level IV (four points each)

10. **BORROWED WORDS** What U.S. mountains have a name that came from the Dutch words for *cats* and *stream*?

11. **HOMOGRAPHS** A big-mouth fish with a deep, booming voice is a ___ ___.

12. **EPONYMS** What U.S. Army infantry weapon has a name that came from that of the city of Bayonne, France in 1704?

Level V (five points each)

13. **BORROWED WORDS** Is the literal French meaning of *pot-pourri* pouring pot, little poor pot, or rotten pot?

14. **EPONYMS** In the 1800s, what type of cracker got its name from that of Sylvester Graham, a man who advised people to eat more coarsely ground whole wheat flour?

15. **GENERAL QUESTIONS** What word in the English language is used more than any other word?

Level VI (six points each)

16. **GENERAL QUESTIONS** How many people in the United States live in homes that speak a language other than English: 1 in 5, 1 in 8, or 1 in 20?

17. **NAMES / NICKNAMES** In 1966, what disparaging,

rhyming, two-word name was coined for *television*?

18. BORROWED WORDS What is the more commonly used synonym for the African Bantu word *goober*?

DID YOU KNOW ...

The Celts called the Germanic invaders of Britain *Saxons*, regardless of whether they were in fact Saxons, Angles, or Jutes.

Angli, from which came *Engle*, which in turn gave rise to *Englisc*, was in use as early as 601 C.E. But *Englaland*, which means *land of the Angles* and is the forerunner of *England*, did not appear until around 1000 C.E.

BETHUMP'D LITE
GAME 2

Level I (one point each)

1. **HOMONYMS** What homonyms are loosely defined as *the voice of a dog* and *the skin of a tree*?

2. **IDIOMS** Which of the following defines what is meant by the expression *The early bird catches the worm*?
   a. early birds get infested with parasites
   b. worms are slow-witted in the morning
   c. those who act first succeed

3. **NAMES / NICKNAMES** What nickname was given to John Chapman after he walked around the United States planting apple seeds?

Level II (two points each)

4. **HOMOPHONES** An ape that is trained to fight jungle warfare is a ___ ___.

5. **PORTMANTEAU WORDS** In 1925, what word was invented by blending the words *motor* and *hotel*?

6. **EPONYMS** What continents' names came from that of Italian navigator and explorer Amerigo Vespucci?

Level III (three points each)

7. **IDIOMS** What are you *up the creek without* if your luck suddenly turns bad?

8. **EPONYMS** In the 1850s, what type of clothing was made first by Levi Strauss?

9. **HOMOPHONES** Alden said, *"In an avalanche, the big fearless rock that races ahead of all the others can be called the ___ ___."*

Level IV (four points each)

10. **BORROWED WORDS** What much too common flowering weed has a name that came from the French words that mean *tooth of the lion*?

11. **IDIOMS** Which of these defines what is meant by *southpaw*?
    - a. a grandfather who lives in the south
    - b. a left-handed person
    - c. the tail of a bear that's walking northward

12. **SLANG** In 1971, what slang term was invented for *food high in calories and low in nutritional value*?

Level V (five points each)

13. **TRUE OR FALSE** English is the mother tongue of the majority of those who live in Quebec, Canada.

14. **BRITICISMS** In Britain, are *dampers* car shocks, rainy days, or wet diapers?

15. **SPOONERISMS** What did college dean William Spooner really mean to say when he said, *"A scoop of boy trouts"*?

Level VI (six points each)

16. HISTORY What economy-vital word was recorded for the first time in America when Thomas Jefferson wrote an essay entitled *Notes on a Money Unit for the United States*?

17. PORTMANTEAU WORDS In 1871, what word did Lewis Carroll coin by blending the words *snort* and *chuckle*?

18. BORROWED WORDS How many states in the United States have names that came from Native American words: 6, 11, or 25?

English is a member of the western branch of the Germanic family of languages, and the Germanic family of languages is a branch of the Indo-European family of languages. Today, the Continental language that is closest to English is Frisian, a Germanic language spoken on the islands and along the coastal regions north of The Netherlands, and in nearby Germany on up to the border of Denmark.

BETHUMP'D LITE
GAME 3

Level I (one point each)

1. **HOMOPHONES** After church on ___, Alicia went to Ben & Jerry's® for a ___.

2. **SPOONERISMS** What did Jackie intend to say when she said, "*The cake had to bake a cook*"?

3. **BORROWED WORDS** Which is the only state in the United States with a Polynesian name?

Level II (two points each)

4. **HOMOGRAPHS** After Mary Jo ___ the magazine, she turned the page to ___ the cover again.

5. **HOMONYMS** Identify the homonyms in this riddle: *The British work to gain it; Americans work to lose it; lovers' hearts do it; stray dogs go to it.*

6. **HISTORY** Who suggested that Native Americans be called *Indians*: George Washington, Christopher Columbus, or Spain's Queen Isabella?

Level III (three points each)

7. **BORROWED WORDS** What musical instrument's name

came from the Hawaiian words *uku*, which means *flea*, and *lele*, which means *jumping*?

8. **HOMOPHONES** Identify the homophones in this sentence: *If Ms Muffet gets her ___ and eats all the curds and ___, she might ___ enough to mash her tuffet.*

9. **EPONYMS** Which of these words came from the name of Guy Fawkes, a man who tried to blow up England's House of Parliament on 4 November 1605: *hawk, fox*, or *guy*?

Level IV (four points each)

10. **PORTMANTEAU WORDS** In 1889, what word was coined by blending the words *electricity* and *execute*?

11. **NAMES / NICKNAMES** What professionals are often called *bean counters* and *number crunchers*?

12. **HOMOPHONES** An ear-tufted wildcat sitting in the middle of the fairway is a ___ on the ___.

Level V (five points each)

13. **ACCENTS** What do Australians mean when they say words that sound like *"Scone ah rhine"*?

14. **HOMOGRAPHS** What homographs are defined as *to tighten by turning* and *an air current stronger than a breeze*?

15. **SLANG** What rhyming term coined in 1943 is often applied as a facetious name for *counterfeit money*?

Level VI (six points each)

16. **ACRONYMS** What do computer geeks mean when they compare the screen to a printout, sigh in relief, and say,

"*Wysiwyg* (wiz-e-wig)"?

17. **WORD ORIGINS** What Latin term means *after noon* and is abbreviated *p.m.*?

18. **BORROWED WORDS** What natives of the cold north were given a name by the Cree Indians that means *eaters of raw flesh*?

DID YOU KNOW ...

About 85% of the words of Old English, our Young Englisc, have long disappeared from use. Today, some 80% of the words most commonly used by speakers of English came from other languages. English, in fact, is far more French than it is Anglo-Saxon. Is it really accurate or even legitimate to call it English?

BETHUMP'D LITE
GAME 4

Level I (one point each)

1. **HOMONYMS** The goofy driver told the police that he thought running his truck back and forth over a huge pile of gourds was a fun way to ___ ___.

2. **PORTMANTEAU WORDS** In 1905, what word was coined by blending the words *fog* and *smoke*?

3. **BORROWED WORDS** In 1884, what name for *ground beef* came from the German word that means *of or from the city of Hamburg*?

Level II (two points each)

4. **IDIOMS** What is meant by the statement *"The trees bit the dust"*?

5. **HOMOGRAPHS** When the bedraggled feline finally climbed out of the well, Katie Jo declared that a cat really ___ nine ___.

6. **EPONYMS** What state was named in honor of the first colonial governor of Virginia, Lord de la Warr?

Level III (three points each)

7. **BRITICISMS** Do the British call *gasoline* auto tonic, go-go juice, or petrol?

8. **HOMOPHONES** A cussing chicken in a rotten mood is a ___-mouthed ___.

9. **SLANG** Are *cheesy* coats those worn by big cheeses, those woven with Swiss cheese-like holes, or shabby?

Level IV (four points each)

10. **LETTER WORDS** What is meant by *SST*, the letter word that describes the French Concord?

11. **BORROWED WORDS** What word came from the Tahitian word that, when first heard, was spelled *t-a-t-a-u* and means *to color the skin*?

12. **ACCENTS** In what part of New York City is *Earl* pronounced *"Oil"* and *oil* pronounced *"earl"*?

Level V (five points each)

13. **SPOONERISMS** What did college dean William Spooner really mean to say when he spluttered the phrase *"a well-boiled icicle"*?

14. **BRITICISMS** What game do the British call *naughts and crosses*?

15. **WORD EVOLUTIONS** Since the Frisian language is close to English, what is the translation of the Frisian expression that is spelled *k-o-p-k-e k-o-f-i-e*?

Level VI (six points each)

16. NAMES / NICKNAMES What Charles Dickens character has a name we can use for *a person who is mean and stingy*?

17. WORD ORIGINS What word is defined as *a wildly foolish person* and came from the Roman belief that behavior is affected by the lunar phases?

18. EUPHEMISMS What actually happened to the 727 that officials of National Airlines formally reported had experienced an *"involuntary conversion"*?

Old English, our Young Englisc, was written in the runic alphabet until some symbols were eliminated when Christian missionaries from Rome partially converted the Anglo-Saxon language to the sound system of the Roman alphabet.

More runic symbols disappeared after the Normans conquered England in 1066, and their scribes began converting English's words to the French version of the Roman alphabet's sound system.

The few remaining runic symbols were not trashed until after the arrival of the printing press. When harried printers could not readily find runic typefaces, they grabbed the closest-sounding Roman symbols, inserted them into place, and printed merrily away, entirely unconcerned with the nuances at stake.

BETHUMP'D LITE
GAME 5

Level I (one point each)

1. **IDIOMS** Is a *sweet tooth* a tasty morsel enjoyed by cannibals, a tooth with a nice disposition, or an appetite for sweet foods?

2. **LETTER WORDS** What letter word is used for the *Federal Bureau of Investigation*?

3. **GENERAL QUESTIONS** What name for a mealtime means *to break one's fast*?

Level II (two points each)

4. **HOMOPHONES** Heather said a person who rents a room in a house that sits on the state line is a ___ ___.

5. **EPONYMS** In the 1840s, what musical instrument was invented by Belgian Antoine Joseph Sax?

6. **BORROWED WORDS** What animal has an Algonquin Indian name that English settlers spelled *a-r-o-u-c-o-u-n*?

Level III (three points each)

7. **GENERAL QUESTIONS** Is the official language of the International Olympics Committee Greek, French, or English?

8. **HOMOGRAPHS** Glenn said that, compared to eternity, a 60-second ___ is a ___ amount of time.

9. **HOMONYMS** What homonyms are loosely defined as *a nocturnal flying mammal* and *a thick stick used to play baseball*?

Level IV (four points each)

10. **EPONYMS** What fruit was distributed by Enoch Bartlett in the early 1800s?

11. **IDIOMS** Which of these defines what is meant by the expression *"He flew the coop"*?
    a. he piloted a flying chicken house
    b. he took a cooper (barrel maker) for a plane ride
    c. he escaped or ran away

12. **HOMOPHONES** Randy claims that a hot and spicy bowl of ___ will warm anyone who lives in the ___ Andes Mountains of ___.

Level V (five points each)

13. **BORROWED WORDS** What 13-mile-long island in New York City has an Amerindian name that means *island mountain*?

14. **BRITICISMS** In Britain, is a *nappy* a diaper, dainty napkin, or short nap before tea time?

15. **WORD ORIGINS** Around 1613, what word was formed by combining the Latin words *solus* and *loqui*, which mean, respectively, *alone* and *to speak*?

Level VI (six points each)

16. CALQUES In 1903, did George Bernard Shaw translate Friedrich Nietzsche's word *Übermensch* into superstar, super-duper, or superman?

17. HISTORY Who was the first to use the term *snow-white*: Geoffrey Chaucer, the brothers Grimm, or Walt Disney?

18. WORD EVOLUTIONS What word meant *stupid* or *foolish* in 1290 but now means *pleasant* or *agreeable*?

English's history is replete with complaints about its ever-changing nature. William Caxton (c.1422-1491), the first to print a book in English, documented one of the most quoted complaints when he related the story of the woman living on the banks of the Thames who, when asked for eggs, thought the speaker was using French.

> "And the marchuant was angry. for he also coude speke no frenshe. but wold haue hadde egges / and she vunderstode hym not / And thenne at laste a nother sayd that he wolde haue eyren / then the good wyf sayd that she vunderstood hym wel / Loo what sholde a man in thyse dayes now wryte. egges or eyren / certaynly it is harde to playse euery man / by cause of dyuersite & chaunge of language."

It seems the good wife was familiar with the Anglo-Saxon word for eggs, *eyren*, but not Norse's *egges*, for which English was beginning to show a preference.

BETHUMP'D LITE
GAME 6

Level I (one point each)

1. **NAMES / NICKNAMES** In 1981, what slang-type name was coined for *a large portable radio and tape player with attached speakers*?

2. **SLANG** In 1982, what term was coined for *a lazy and, usually, overeating person who spends too much time watching TV*?

3. **HOMOPHONES** Country doctors who went to homes and spent time with the ill had more ___ with their ___.

Level II (two points each)

4. **WORD EVOLUTIONS** In the days before dictionaries brought greater stability to spellings, what word was spelled *l-i-e-i-f, l-i-e-f,* and *l-e-f-e*?

5. **HOMOPHONES** A reasonably priced airline ticket is a ___ ___.

6. **IDIOMS** What idiom could be misinterpreted to mean *common house pets are falling from the sky*?

Level III (three points each)

7. BORROWED WORDS What state's name came from the Cherokee Indian word for *villages*, which early explorers phonetically spelled *t-a-n-a-s-i*?

8. HISTORY Although eggs have been consumed by humans since the dawn of time, what stellar term for preparing them did not appear in English until about 1901?

9. PORTMANTEAU WORDS In 1964, what words were blended to form the word *sitcom*?

Level IV (four points each)

10. AUSTRALIANISMS In Australia, is a *dingo* a dim-witted person, wild dog, or tiny bell?

11. BORROWED WORDS In 1944, what word came from the German word spelled *S-c-h-n-o-r-c-h-e-l*?

12. HISTORY Is the rate of growth of English's vocabulary slowing, remaining constant, or accelerating?

Level V (five points each)

13. BORROWED WORDS In 1670, what name for *a rider of horses* was borrowed from Scandinavian where it is used as a nickname for *John*?

14. WORD EVOLUTIONS In the 16th century, was a *tomboy* a rude and boisterous girl, boy, or both?

15. WORD ORIGINS What city in Quebec, Canada has a name that means *Mount Royal* in French?

Level VI (six points each)

16. IDIOMS What idiom came from the Latin expression *tempus fugit*?

17. WORD ORIGINS What related words evolved out of the names *Moon, Tiu, Woden, Thor, Frig, Saturn,* and *Sun?*

18. CALQUES What part of New York City once had a Dutch name that was spelled *V-l-a-c-h-t b-o-s-c-h* and means *level forest?*

It seems every generation is convinced the next is hell-bent on destroying the English language, and one day will succeed. In 1712, Jonathan Swift lamented: Our Language's "daily Improvements are by no means in proportion to its daily Corruptions; ...the Pretenders to polish and refine it, have chiefly multiplied Abuses and Absurdities... "

Like many others through history—John Dryden, Daniel Defoe, John Quincy Adams, Noah Webster, and on up to those of today—Swift believed the force of law was necessary to defend and save the language from certain ruin. Also like the others, he proposed the creation of an Academy of English. But his proposal, like those before and since, garnered little support and English continued to race untethered into the future, oblivious of the commotion. Despite Swift's fretting, the language's ability today to communicate changing and increasingly complex thought with precision far surpasses that of the past.

BETHUMP'D LITE
GAME 7

Level I (one point each)

1. **WORD EVOLUTIONS** Back when Old English was spoken, what time of the day was known as *mórgen*?

2. **HOMOPHONES** Alfred said, "If Mister Ed's vocal cords get sore from too much talking he'll sound like a ___ ___."

3. **HOMOGRAPHS** When a gardener grows more than she can eat, she ___ ___ what is left over for meals in the winter.

Level II (two points each)

4. **EPONYMS** What state has a Latinized name honoring King George II?

5. **IDIOMS** What games were played by the person who *aced a hole* and, later, had *an ace in the hole*?

6. **BORROWED WORDS** What language borrowed an American phrase and translated it into *ein Image Problem*?

Level III (three points each)

7. **BRITICISMS** In Britain, is a *lift* a free ride into town, a refreshing drink of tea, or an elevator?

8. **HOMONYMS** What homonyms are defined as *a tart green fruit* and *a finely-ground calcinaceous rock that is used to 'sweeten' the soil*?

9. **BORROWED WORDS** *Bambi* is a name derived from *bambino*, which means *little child* in Italian, French, or German?

Level IV (four points each)

10. **EUPHEMISMS** What, in plain English, is *a recycled auto center*?

11. **BORROWED WORDS** In 1679, what word came from the Dutch word that is spelled *b-a-a-s* and means *master*?

12. **HOMONYMS** What homonyms are defined as *a rigid cardboard container* and *to fight with gloved fists*?

Level V (five points each)

13. **EPONYMS** Some believe Jonas the Dutchman, whose family name was spelled *B-r-o-n-c-k*, once had a farm in what part of New York City?

14. **BRITICISMS** In Britain, is a *flat* an apartment, a five-pound note, or a potato pancake?

15. **GENERAL QUESTIONS** Is more Irish or English spoken in Ireland?

Level VI (six points each)

16. **IDIOMS** What parts of the body are used to pay for something that is outrageously expensive?

17. **WORD ORIGINS** What huge barrel-shaped animal spends most of its life in water and got its name from the Greek

words that mean *horse of the river*?

18. HISTORY In 1941, what name for the 26 nations that were at war with Germany, Italy, and Japan was coined by President Franklin D. Roosevelt?

DID YOU KNOW ...

Workers' attempts to make their jobs easier played a powerful role in the development of key aspects of today's English. The early Roman alphabet, for one of numerous examples, contained 23 letters, all of which were capitals. Capital letters were a time-consuming pain for scribes because, not only were they big and required a lot of ink, the pen had to be lifted from the paper between the writing of each. The routine was monotonous. Dip the tip of the pen in ink, put it to the paper, lift it, put it to the paper, lift it, dip it in ink, put it to the paper, lift it, and so on through some really long-winded stuff. And, as soon as the ink dried on the last letter, the boss invariably waltzed in and asked for ten copies to pass on to friends.

The problem led the weary and frustrated scribes to develop a system of high-speed writing wherein the pen only left the paper between *words*, and less ink and inkwell dipping was required. Thanks to their interest in making their jobs easier, we now have lower case letters and the highly efficient cursive style.

BETHUMP'D LITE
GAME 8

Level I (one point each)

1. **HOMOPHONES** When the traveling bumpkin got home, he ran to his friend Charlie and said, *"Good golly, Cholly, in the hotel a ___ actually ___ my bed."*

2. **EPONYMS** What invention was introduced in 1867 by Samuel F.B. Morse?

3. **BORROWED WORDS** In 1806, what name for *a small cube of crisply fried bread* was borrowed from French?

Level II (two points each)

4. **IDIOMS** Which of these explains what kids do whose *eyes are bigger than their stomachs*?
   a. they see fantastic distances
   b. with stomachs so tiny, they get skinny
   c. they take more food than they can eat

5. **NAMES / NICKNAMES** What U.S. city is known as the *Mile-High City*?

6. **HOMOPHONES** Her father ___ her how to keep her line ___ when she caught a fish.

Level III (three points each)

7. **BORROWED WORDS** What word came from the Greek word that is spelled *k-a-t-á-l-o-g-o-s*?

8. **IDIOMS** In many idioms, what non-food item is often called *bread, pork, beans,* or *bacon*?

9. **EPONYMS** In 1824, what material used to build roads was named after its inventor, John L. McAdam, a British engineer?

Level IV (four points each)

10. **LETTER WORDS** What information processing machine is known by the letter word *PC*?

11. **EPONYMS** What state was named in honor of France's King Louis XIV?

12. **IDIOMS** What type of broad grin is named after that of an animal's in Lewis Carroll's *Alice's Adventures in Wonderland*?

Level V (five points each)

13. **BRITICISMS** In Britain, are *wellies* little water wells, recovering hospital patients, or rubber boots?

14. **BORROWED WORDS** In 1825, what word was borrowed from Dharuk, an Australian aboriginal language, for *a wing-like throwing club that curves in the air and comes back to the thrower*?

15. **BRITICISMS** In Britain, are *crisps* fried bacon strips, potato chips, or sunburned swimmers?

Level VI (six points each)

16. EUPHEMISMS What, in plain English, is *post-consumer secondary material*?

17. WORD ORIGINS What generic name for animals that live on land *and* in the water came from the Greek word that means *living a double life*?

18. HISTORY Based on its earliest documented appearance, the use of *ain't* began sometime around 1778 but, because it represents a 'corrupted usage', lexicographers refused to add it to dictionaries until 1953, 1973, or 1993?

DID YOU KNOW ...

When it comes to articulation, the letter *t* is one of the letters of the alphabet that is least voiced by speakers of American English. While most educated speakers of British English make a clearly heard distinction between each word in word pairs like *latter* and *ladder*, *waiting* and *wading*, and *writing* and *riding*, the same words come out as *t*-less *d*-containing homophones in the speech of most bread and *budder*-eating Americans.

BETHUMP'D LITE
GAME 9

Level I (one point each)

1. **HOMOPHONES** At the circus, Katie Jo ___ a ball ___ the smallest hoop and won a giant teddy bear.

2. **LETTER WORDS** What is known by the letter word *POW*?

3. **EPONYMS** Name the bell that was put up in London in 1856 by Benjamin Hall.

Level II (two points each)

4. **PORTMANTEAU WORDS** What word that is very important to the English language is a portmanteau of the Greek words *alpha* and *beta*?

5. **EPONYMS** What nut was discovered by Australian chemist John Macadam?

6. **BORROWED WORDS** What word came from the Norse word that is spelled *s-k-i-t-h* and means *stick of wood*?

Level III (three points each)

7. **BRITICISMS** Do the British call *french fries* spudlettes, chips, or waterloos?

8. **IDIOMS** Which of the following defines what is meant by the statement *"Life is like a bowl of cherries"*?
   a. life is full of pits
   b. hang out with the crowd and you'll get mashed, baked, and eaten
   c. life is enjoyable

9. **PORTMANTEAU WORDS** In 1996, what dialect of English was at the center of an emotional controversy after the Oakland, California School District called it *"a legitimate language"*?

Level IV (four points each)

10. **NAMES / NICKNAMES** In the presidential campaign of 1996, what sport was supported by the mothers who suddenly found themselves part of a voting block important to politicians?

11. **HOMOPHONES** Identify the homophones in the riddle: *Cobblers work to shape it; doctors work to do it.*

12. **BRITICISMS** In Britain, is *candy floss* a sweetened dental thread, a sweet but meaningless remark, or cotton candy?

Level V (five points each)

13. **EPONYMS** In 1537, what name was given to the fortune tellers wandering through Europe who were erroneously thought to have come from Egypt?

14. **WORD ORIGINS** What word that means *fear of heights* came from the Greek words *akros* and *phobia*, which mean *at the top* and *fear of*?

15. **TRUE OR FALSE** The use of the word *pooped* to mean *exhausted* started in the groovy lingo days of the 1960s.

Level VI (six points each)

16. HISTORY Was the first free U.S. public library founded by Noah Webster, George Washington, or Benjamin Franklin?

17. BORROWED WORDS The -*a-g-e* ending of words like band*age*, voy*age*, camoufl*age*, and gar*age* is a strong signal they were borrowed from what language?

18. CANADIANISMS In Canada, what is a *Molson's muscle*?

In 1642, Puritans in Britain forced Shakespeare's Globe theater into permanent closure because they concluded his plays were vulgar and sinful. The building was demolished.

BETHUMP'D LITE
GAME 10

Level I (one point each)

1. **WORD EVOLUTIONS** What word that is used when departing came from the 16th century expression *"God be with ye"*?

2. **HOMOPHONES** It would be an amazing and thunderous ___ if an elephant leaped six ___ in the air.

3. **HOMOGRAPHS** What homographs are defined as *nearby* and *to shut*?

Level II (two points each)

4. **GENERAL QUESTIONS** Which has the most influence over the way words are spelled: teachers, television, newspapers, novels, dictionaries, or magazines?

5. **LETTER WORDS** What is meant by the letter word *TGIF*?

6. **NAMES / NICKNAMES** What country's citizens are known around the world as *Yankees*?

Level III (three points each)

7. **BORROWED WORDS** If the Spanish word *nevar* means *to snow*, what state's name came from the Spanish word for

snowy?

8. **LETTER WORDS** What government agency is known as the *CIA*?

9. **IDIOMS** Which of the following explains what is meant by the statement *"She's as fit as a fiddle"*?
    a. she has excellent health
    b. all her promises have strings attached
    c. her voice is strong and high-pitched

Level IV (four points each)

10. **AMERICANISMS** In 1888, what title was coined for *a person who, through competition, is ranked among the best in the United States*?

11. **SLANG** In 1852, what slang term was coined for *newspaper comics*?

12. **BRITICISMS** In Britain, is *a car's boot* its front bumper, right rear tire, or trunk?

Level V (five points each)

13. **EPONYMS** What word is used almost every morning and came from the name Ceres, the Roman goddess of agriculture?

14. **ACRONYMS** What government organization is known by the acronym *NASA*?

15. **PORTMANTEAU WORDS** In 1977, what name was coined for the car fuel that combines *alcohol* and *gasoline*?

16. AUSTRALIANISMS In Australia, is a *dill* an ill dog, a tart remark, or a foolish person?

17. HOMONYMS Identify the homonyms in the riddle: *Musicians test it; ships do it; slopes have it; conifers make it.*

18. WORD ORIGINS In 1926, was the word *zipper* coined by the editors of *Merriam-Webster's Collegiate Dictionary*, the B.F. Goodrich Company, or H.L. Mencken?

English's addiction to borrowing words from other languages has unnerved purists for centuries. In 1557, John Cheke expressed what is now recognized as the usual complaint:

> "I am of this opinion that our tung shold be written cleane and pure, vnmixt and vnmangeled with borowing of other tunges, wherein if we take not heed bi tijm, euer borowing and neuer payeing, she shall be fain to keep her house as bankrupt."

English, of course, has grown rich and strong from borrowing, and has been encouraged to do even more by the likes of Cheke's contemporary Thomas Elyot, the 20th century's H.L. Mencken, and many others. Cheke's use of *bankrupt* is interesting, too, in that it is a word English borrowed from Italian. In fact, it is quite difficult to complain about English's word borrowing without using borrowed words, especially if you try to express it in a form that's original.

BETHUMP'D LITE
GAME 11

Level I (one point each)

1. **BORROWED WORDS** In about 1838, what word came from the German word that is spelled *B-r-e-z-e-l* and means *a brittle salted bread*?

2. **HOLORIMIC PHRASES** What other phrase might be heard when someone says, *"Isle of view"*?

3. **IDIOMS** Is *a person who always finds ways for others to pay his expenses* called a lemon, sponge, or fruitcake?

Level II (two points each)

4. **HOMOPHONES** What homophones are defined as *fixed looks* and *flights of steps*?

5. **LETTER WORDS** From the words of what language did English derive the letter word *RSVP*?

6. **BRITICISMS** In Britain, is a *creepie* a little creep, a low stool, or a baby who is yet to walk?

Level III (three points each)

7. **HOMOGRAPHS** What homographs are defined as *a gift* and *to introduce*?

8. **AMERICANISMS** When something is done in an impressively nonchalant way, what temperature-related word is used by hip kids in statements like *"Man, that was ___ "*?

9. **ACCENTS** What do Australians mean when they ask a question that sounds like *"Emma chisit"*?

Level IV (four points each)

10. **SLANG** In the 1960s, what name was given to *performances involving rhythmic monotone chanting in rhymed couplets to a musical beat*?

11. **HOMOPHONES** Identify the homophones in the riddle: *Some wear them tight to the skin; all carry them in cells of the skin.*

12. **BORROWED WORDS** In 1857, what word came from the Japanese word for *top leader* and at first was phonetically spelled *t-a-i-k-u-n*?

Level V (five points each)

13. **BRITICISMS** In Britain, are *hairgrips* Irish hair-pulling contests, bobby pins, or mohair suitcases?

14. **TRUE OR FALSE** In the 13th century, a *shrew* was a mean and wicked woman.

15. **EPONYMS** In 1897, what slang term came into English from the name of the whiskey-making Hoochinoo Indians?

Level VI (six points each)

16. **WORD EVOLUTIONS** What word was spelled *g-i-c-e-l* 1,000 years ago, *i-k-y-l* 600 years ago, and *i-c-k-l-e* 400 years ago?

17. AUSTRALIANISMS When an Australian says something is *dinkum*, does she mean it's stupid, honest, or smells rotten and should be dunked?

18. NAMES / NICKNAMES What title is proudly worn by both mafia leaders and distinguished members of the staff at Oxford University?

DID YOU KNOW ...

The 18th century's Samuel Johnson, universally acclaimed as one of history's greatest lexicographers, wrote some of the most subjective definitions ever to appear in a dictionary. Here are two of his more well-known.

> **LEXICOGRAPHER** A writer of dictionaries; a harmless drudge, that busies himself in tracing the original, and detailing the signification of words.

> **OATS** A grain, which in England is generally given to horses, but in Scotland supports the people.

BETHUMP'D LITE
GAME 12

Level I (one point each)

1. **IDIOMS** What single word completes these idiomatic statements?
   a. They ____ me up the wall.
   b. They're going to ____ me nuts.
   c. They always ____ a hard bargain.

2. **HOMOGRAPHS** When Robin's arrow hit the bull's-eye, he unstrung his ____ and turned to Marian, grinned, and took an exaggerated ____.

3. **EPONYMS** In 1899, what knitting pattern got its name from Archibald Campbell, third duke of Argyll?

Level II (two points each)

4. **HOMONYMS** Identify the homonyms in the riddle: *A lion leads it; a mother has it.*

5. **EPONYMS** In 1956, what luncheon preparation was invented and introduced by American grocer Reuben Kulakofsky?

6. **SPOONERISMS** What did William Spooner really intend to say when he said, That's "*a blushing crow*"?

Level III (three points each)

7. **BORROWED WORDS** What animal in Florida was named *el lagarto* because Spanish explorers thought it was a lizard?

8. **ACCENTS** What breakfast food do you serve an Australian who asks for *"Emma necks"*?

9. **BORROWED WORDS** In 1891, what word was borrowed from Finnish for *a bath that is made by pouring water on hot rocks*?

Level IV (four points each)

10. **AMERICANISMS** On U.S. college campuses, what culinary disappointment is known as *a circle of death*?

11. **HOMOPHONES** A poet banned from performing in public is a ___ ___.

12. **BRITICISMS** In Britain, is a *jumper* a hound trained for fox hunts, a sweater, or a frightfully large flea found in the Highlands?

Level V (five points each)

13. **BORROWED WORDS** In 1848, what word was borrowed from German that is defined as *a mischievous ghost that makes noise by knocking and throwing things around*?

14. **TRUE OR FALSE** About 600 years ago, little boys were called girls.

15. **BRITICISMS** In Britain, is a *hoover* a hooves-using glue-maker, descendant of Herbert Hoover, or vacuum cleaner?

Level VI (six points each)

16. **PORTMANTEAU WORDS**   In Louisiana, is *a turkey stuffed with duck stuffed with chicken* called a turducken, duchic-in-a-turk, or a tuduchick?

17. **LINGUISTICS**   What symbols represent sounds and are called *phonograms* by linguists?

18. **ACRONYMS**   What does Disney World's *EPCOT* stand for?

Language is a personal and ofttimes emotional issue for many, especially when challenged by literary critics or overly punctilious grammarians. This excerpt is from a letter written to the editor of London's *Chronicle* in 1892, and is one of the more colorful reactions to a language critic.

"If you do not immediately suppress the person who takes it upon himself to lay down the law almost every day in your columns on the subject of literary composition, I will give up the *Chronicle*. The man is a pedant, an ignoramus, an idiot and a self-advertising duffer. ...Set him adrift and try an intelligent Newfoundland dog in his place."

George Bernard Shaw

GAME 13

Level I (one point each)

1. **AMERICANISM** What Americanism evolved out of the expression *"How do ye"*?

2. **HOMOPHONES** A man with loose false teeth must carefully ___ what he ___.

3. **EPONYMS** What part of certain male hairstyles got its name from Civil War General Ambrose E. Burnside?

Level II (two points each)

4. **HOMOPHONES** Identify and spell the homophones defined as *lacking resources*, *to flow easily*, and *a tiny opening in the skin*?

5. **LETTER WORDS** What group likes to putt around and is known as the *PGA*?

6. **IDIOMS** Idiomatically speaking, what value is placed on *a bird in the hand*?

Level III (three points each)

7. **BRITICISMS** In Britain, is a *torch* a flamethrower, match, or flashlight?

8. **HOMOGRAPHS** When the dump filled to capacity, the gate attendant said he had to ___ taking any more ___.

9. **SLANG** Is a person who talks about his or her *main squeeze* referring to their preferred fruit juice, style of handshake, or lover?

Level IV (four points each)

10. **EPONYMS** What month got its name from the title Rome bestowed on Caesar in 27 B.C.E.?

11. **HISTORY** In the early 20th century, was the world's third largest German-speaking population found in Frankfurt, London, or New York City?

12. **NAMES / NICKNAMES** During the presidential campaign of 1996, which of these names did Republican candidate Robert Dole bestow on Democratic President Bill Clinton's White House: *Animal House*, *Waffle House*, or *Arkansas-East*?

Level V (five points each)

13. **WORD ORIGINS** Which of these sources of many common English words gave rise to *aspirin*, *cornflakes*, and *nylon*: Latin, slang, or trademarks?

14. **AUSTRALIANISMS** What slang term is known to Australian comedians as *The Great Australian Adjective*?

15. **HOMOPHONES** What homophones are defined as *24 sheets of typing paper* and *a harmonic group*?

Level VI (six points each)

16. **EUPHEMISMS** What do politicians call the effort they put into minimizing the harm done by their publicly exposed mis-

takes?

17. **WORD ORIGINS**   While many people have coined from one to as many as a dozen words in their lifetimes, did Shakespeare coin 35-50, 60-85, or 1,700-1,800?

18. **WORD ORIGINS**   What word is defined as *a navigable, iconic 3D interface that represents all the world's data* and was coined in 1982 by science fiction writer William Gibson?

English's irregular spellings have evoked calls for reform and outbursts of criticism through the ages. Comedians find them particularly tempting targets.

"I hold that a man has just as mutch rite tew spel a word as it is pronounced, as he has tew pronounce it the way it ain't spelt."

Henry Wheeler Shaw
aka *Josh Billings*
1868

BETHUMP'D LITE
GAME 14

Level I (one point each)

1. **IDIOMS** What bird's flight is commonly used to refer to *the shortest distance between two points*?

2. **HOMOPHONES** Whenever the Holstein got hungry, she got into a terrible ___ and usually ___ loud and endlessly, until old MacDonald fed her some grain and hay.

3. **EPONYMS** In 1767, what flower was named in honor of Johann G. Zinn?

Level II (two points each)

4. **SLANG** What is held in common by the words *slammer*, *clink*, *hoosegow*, and *pokey*?

5. **HOMOPHONES** The donkey ___ until Jess untied the ___ in its tail.

6. **PORTMANTEAU WORDS** What word is a blend of the Latin words *super* and *sonus*, which means *sound*?

Level III (three points each)

7. **TRUE OR FALSE** In 1947, the word *honcho* was borrowed from German where it means *squad leader*.

8. **BRITICISMS** In Britain, is *a car's hood* called a mechanic's door, motor cap, or bonnet?

9. **BORROWED WORDS** What word came from the Czech word that is spelled *p-í-š-t-à-l-a* and means *pipe* or *fife*?

Level IV (four points each)

10. **EPONYMS** What word is defined as *one who is slow-witted* and came from the middle name of John *Duns* Scotus, a late 13th to early 14th century theologian whose once accepted writings were later ridiculed?

11. **NAMES / NICKNAMES** What nickname was given to the long-range cannon made by Germany's Krupp Munitions Works during the time it was managed by Bertha Krupp?

12. **BORROWED WORDS** What word reached English in 1551, long after it originated in the Arabic words that are spelled *a-l* and *j-a-b-r* and mean *the reduction*?

Level V (five points each)

13. **HOMOPHONES** Identify and spell three words that are homophones of Wilbur and Orville's family name.

14. **WORD EVOLUTIONS** What word was once defined as *a sweetheart, a fine chap* and is now used to mean *a blustering brow-beater*?

15. **QUOTATIONS** Did Henry Wadsworth Longfellow call poetry, money, or music *"the universal language of mankind"*?

Level VI (six points each)

16. **BORROWED WORDS** What state's name did Hernando Cortés get out of the poem *Las Sergas de Esplandián*, which

describes an island rich in gold and inhabited by Amazon-like women?

17. **IDIOMS** Which of these authors coined the idioms *dead broke*, *to get even*, *a close call*, and *take it easy*: Dr. Seuss, Mark Twain, or Carolyn Keene?

18. **WORD ORIGINS** In 1516, what name was coined by Thomas More for *an imaginary country inhabited by people who developed an ideal society*?

The genealogy of our alphabet traces back to the North Semitic alphabet, which was invented about 3,700 years ago and is the oldest known. The trail of evolution leads from the North Semitics to the Phoenicians, moves on to the Greeks, and from there, about 2,800 years ago, to the Etruscans of the Tuscany region of central Italy. The Etruscan modifications of the alphabet led to the early Roman alphabet.

BETHUMP'D LITE
GAME 15

Level I (one point each)

1. **HOMOPHONES** An effective repellant collar will make a ___ ___ a dog for parts unknown.

2. **LETTER WORDS** What letter word is used to mean *extrasensory perception*?

3. **HOMOPHONES** The emotional young man ___ for an hour after he combed his hair and discovered he was going ___.

Level II (two points each)

4. **ACCENTS** In Brooklyn, what is meant when a native says, *"Goils love oily boids"*?

5. **HOMOGRAPHS** What homographs are defined as *a salty secretion of an eye* and *to rip apart*?

6. **IDIOMS** Is a person who cries *at the drop of a hat* a hat fanatic, terrified of hats, or overly emotional?

Level III (three points each)

7. **GLOBAL ENGLISH** In what European country do the young often refer to something that is awesome with the expression *"C'est fun mega-top cool"*?

8. **BORROWED WORDS** In 1513, Ponce de León used the Spanish word for *flowery* to name what part of North America?

9. **HOLORIMIC PHRASES** What other phrase is heard in the 1940s song title that is spelled *M-a-i-r-z-y D-o-a-t-s*?

Level IV (four points each)

10. **BRITICISMS** In Britain, if a man buys a *silencer* is he planning a murder, to poach game on Royal lands, or to quiet his car?

11. **HOMOPHONES** The burglars knew the owner did not use banks, so they searched until they found a ___ of ___ stashed in bags behind a fake wall.

12. **SLANG** In the 1930s, did jive-talking Cab Calloway define *jail key* as a twister to the slammer, klink-linker, or pokey rod?

Level V (five points each)

13. **ACRONYMS** What military unit is known by the acronym *MASH*?

14. **HISTORY** Of the fifty states in the United States, which is the only with a name honoring a person of European ancestry who was born in America?

15. **BORROWED WORDS** What word literally means *acidulous cabbage* in German?

Level VI (six points each)

16. **EPONYMS** In 1945, what antibiotic was isolated from microbes discovered in the tissues of little Margaret Tracy?

17. **ACRONYMS** What is known to determined and aggressive land developers as a *NIMBY*?

18. **GENERAL QUESTIONS** About what percent of the world's scientists publish their research in English: 8, 13, or 67?

DID YOU KNOW ...

The purpose of punctuation is to clarify meaning. Its purpose is to enhance the words' ability to accurately convey the writer's thoughts.

Before the Renaissance, however, punctuation marks were used to indicate the location and timing of pauses, and even the breathing of those who might read the writing aloud. The use of marks like periods and colons was haphazard at best, and had no relationship to the way we use them today. It was not uncommon earliertoevenencounterwritingswherethescribedid- notleavespacesbetweenwords. There is no doubt that our ability to communicate in written form has improved immensely.

BETHUMP'D LITE
GAME 16

Level I (one point each)

1. **BORROWED WORDS** In German, if *zwie* means *twice* and *backen* means *to bake*, what are *zwieback cookies*?

2. **HOMOPHONES** Due to an unusually heavy morning ___, two trucks ___ the turn and skidded out of control.

3. **NAMES / NICKNAMES** What stadium seats were given a name as a direct result of the sun's ability to oxidize colors?

Level II (two points each)

4. **HOMOPHONES** For the noise-loving kids in the band's percussion section, the ___ were status ___.

5. **BRITICISMS** Do the British call *a tour bus* a coach, lorry, or grey dog?

6. **DINOSAUR WORDS** Is Ms Muffet's *tuffet* a mushroom, suitcase, or stool?

Level III (three points each)

7. **IDIOMS** Is a person who is *off their rocker* a recovered rocking chair addict, an escaped grandparent, or crazy?

8. **PORTMANTEAU WORDS** What computer device's name is a blend of the words *modulate* and *demodulate*?

9. **EPONYMS** What word came from the name of mythological King Tantalus, who embarrassed the gods and was condemned to Hades where he was tormented by food and water that was kept slightly out his reach?

Level IV (four points each)

10. **AMERICANISMS** On U.S. college campuses, how do students define the word *momouflage*?

11. **LETTER WORDS** What entertainment company is known by the letter word *MGM*?

12. **IDIOMS** What idiom means *a no-win situation* and came from the title of a 1961 novel by Joseph Heller?

Level V (five points each)

13. **BORROWED WORDS** In French, does *Mardi Gras* mean many thanks, March grass, or fat Tuesday?

14. **HOMOPHONES** A person who accurately predicts what is left over after all expenses are paid is a ___ ___.

15. **NAMES / NICKNAMES** Do linguists call *the English used by the International Civil Aviation Association* plain talk, aerodrone, or airspeak?

Level VI (six points each)

16. **AMERICANISMS** What name for a type of meat product appeared in American English around 1900 and was later defined by H.L. Mencken as "*a cartridge filled with the sweepings of abbatoirs*"?

17. BORROWED WORDS In 1535, what country was inadvertently named *village* because explorer Jacques Cartier happen to wave in the direction of a settlement when he asked his Indian guide what the *area* was called?

18. HISTORY In 1978, which of these conclusions was drawn on the words *viable, relevant,* and *ongoing* by Britain's House of Lords?
   a. they are useful in very few situations
   b. they are language-cluttering monstrosities
   c. they are ingenious inventions

DID YOU KNOW ...

Printers of the 15th and later centuries often arbitrarily changed the spelling of the last words on lines, adding or dropping letters, in order to keep the right-hand margin straight and neat in appearance. Many printers were not well educated or were foreign users of English and, thus, were also prone to spelling mistakes and inconsistencies. Since a large number of authors suffered similar shortcomings, some manuscripts from the period personify orthographic chaos.

BETHUMP'D LITE
GAME 17

Level I (one point each)

1. **HOMOPHONES** The gardener let out a ___ when he saw his peas had not ___ an inch as a result of the dry weather.

2. **EPONYMS** What month got its name in 44 B.C.E. from that of Julius Caesar?

3. **TRUE OR FALSE** The *teddy bear* was named after Teddy Roosevelt who, when hunting in 1906, saved a bear cub's life.

Level II (two points each)

4. **BORROWED WORDS** In 1717, what word came from the Arabic word for *long bench* and was first spelled *s-u-f-f-a-h*?

5. **TRUE OR FALSE** The words *blues, boogie-woogie, jive,* and *ragtime* were coined by African-Americans.

6. **HOMOPHONES** Identify and spell the homophones in this sentence: *He ___ a bike along the ___, then ___ a boat across the lake.*

Level III (three points each)

7. **IDIOMS** What is a skater planning if she says she is going to *break the ice* with a new friend: vandalism, a wild skating

party, or starting a relationship?

8. **EPONYMS** What geological formation got its name from Vulcan, the Roman god of fire?

9. **HOMOPHONES** Every day at noon, the bucks move into the woods while the ___ ___ in the sun.

Level IV (four points each)

10. **BRITICISMS** In Britain, is a person who is said to be *dressed up like a dog's dinner* wearing grubby, flashy, or plain clothes?

11. **ACCENTS** Which of these TV newsmen took elocution lessons to eliminate his Texan accent: Dan Rather, Peter Jennings, or Tom Brokaw?

12. **BORROWED WORDS** What Choctaw Indian word for *marsh* was initially spelled *b-a-y-u-k* by the Louisiana French?

Level V (five points each)

13. **AUSTRALIANISMS** In Australia, is *yakka* corny jokes, hard work, or gossip?

14. **GENERAL QUESTIONS** How many letters are in the Japanese alphabet: zero, 27, or 96?

15. **BRITICISMS** In Britain, is *the second floor of a building* called the first floor, the over-floor, or the one-up?

Level VI (six points each)

16. **BORROWED WORDS** What Italian greeting appeared in English in 1929 and literally means *I am your slave*?

17. HOMOGRAPHS What homographs are defined as *to cut down* and *the place in a barn where hay is stored*?

18. WORD ORIGINS In 1533, what word came into English from French after originating in Latin and passing through Italian where it was written as the combination of *banca* (bank) + *rotta* (broken)?

English once followed the German tradition of capitalizing nouns as well as the first letter at the beginning of each sentence. In addition, some early writers even capitalized the first letter at the beginning of each *line*. Our present approach to capitalization—which the reading of any daily newspaper shows is only less inconsistent—evolved over time and was essentially in place by the early 19th century.

In 1789, Benjamin Franklin complained to Noah Webster that the change from the German practice lowered reading comprehension. He blamed the desire to change on "the fancy of printers," who believed they were showing the letters of their printed material to greater advantage by not disturbing the even, regular appearance of lines with mid-stream insertions of large capital letters.

BETHUMP'D LITE
GAME 18

Level I (one point each)

1. **HOMONYMS** What homonyms are defined as *the baseball player at the plate* and *a mixture of flour, eggs, and milk*?

2. **JARGON** What sport was Francis playing when he *made a bucket*?

3. **HOMOPHONES** What homophones are defined as *the sound of a chick* and *not costly*?

Level II (two points each)

4. **EPONYMS** What is the family name of Louis ___, the person who developed a system of writing for the blind in 1853?

5. **HOMOPHONES** The circus boss said he would grill ___ for the boys to eat after they finished pounding in all the ___ of the big tent.

6. **IDIOMS** In the 19th century, Alfred, Lord Tennyson, coined *"Ring out the old, ring in the new,"* an idiom that is used repeatedly at what time of year?

Level III (three points each)

7. **TRUE OR FALSE** The word *car* made its first appearance

in English in the 19th century.

8. **EPONYMS** Did the words *calico, satin,* and *cashmere* come from peoples' names, cities' names, or trademarks?

9. **SLANG** What term is used to mean *tramp* in Australia, *traveling salesman* in Britain, and *collector of illicit money* in the United States?

Level IV (four points each)

10. **BRITICISMS** In Britain, is a *drawing pin* the pin of a hand grenade, an artist's tool for drawing circles, or a thumbtack?

11. **BORROWED WORDS** What is the literal French meaning of *cul-de-sac?*

12. **BRITICISMS** In Britain, is a *cheeky* person someone who is always smiling, has jowly cheeks, or is impudent?

Level V (five points each)

13. **EPONYMS** What weapon did Robert Fulton name after *a fish that is capable of giving electric shocks?*

14. **WORD EVOLUTIONS** In what year was *rap* defined as *to talk freely*: 1929, 1969, or 1989?

15. **TRUE OR FALSE** George I, king of England from 1714 to 1727, was known for his articulate and eloquent English.

Level VI (six points each)

16. **HISTORY** In 1873, what new machine was Mark Twain excited about when he wrote: *"It piles an awful stack of words on one page"*?

17. CALQUES   What name for a type of market is a direct translation of the French words *Marché aux Puces*?

18. WORD ORIGINS   In 1943, did the word *gunk* come from a portmanteau of gun and junk, a trademark, or a portmanteau of gunny and sack?

DID YOU KNOW ...

While printers and publishers are blamed for a number of oddities that have crept into the English language, their early colleagues are credited with 'discovering' the value of *alphabetical order*.

In the Middle Ages, few saw much advantage to alphabetizing lists of words. If it was done at all, most thought it sufficient to dump all words that begin with the same letter into the same pile, the *a*-words into one *scrambled* pile, the *b*-words into another *scrambled* pile, and so on.

Medieval printers, of course, had the same attitude until they realized how much time was wasted searching through piles of typefaces for letters, and through similarly scrambled glossaries for the spellings of words. It was a momentous stroke of genius when they finally put their typefaces in trays arranged in alphabetical order, and gradually did the same with their glossaries.

But this was merely the beginning. Alphabetization as *a working concept*, as a methodic way to enhance the efficiency of dealing with any and all compilations of words, did not begin to develop in the community at-large until the advent of more modern dictionaries.

GAME 19

Level I (one point each)

1. **ACCENTS** Where is an Australian going if he says he's attending a meeting of *"the tan cancel"*?

2. **HOMOPHONES** A 3-year-old female horse from Philadelphia is a ___ from ___.

3. **BORROWED WORDS** What word came from the Dutch word that is spelled *S-i-n-t-e-r-k-l-a-a-s?*

Level II (two points each)

4. **HOMOPHONES** What homophones are defined as *a processed grain breakfast food* and *a story appearing in sequential parts*?

5. **BORROWED WORDS** What word used by ski buffs came from a Viennese word that is spelled *m-u-g-l* and means *little hill*?

6. **ACCENTS** In Australia, what is meant when someone says, *"Aorta do it"*?

Level III (three points each)

7. **HOMOGRAPHS** What homographs are defined as *to com-*

fort and *the housing for the controlling dials and switches*?

8. **EUPHEMISMS** Are employees who are *downsized* demoted, fired, or forced to wear shorter heels?

9. **NAMES / NICKNAMES** Which of these newspapers do journalists refer to as *McPaper*: *The Dublin Times, Boston Globe, USA Today*?

Level IV (four points each)

10. **PORTMANTEAU WORDS** In 1651, what word did John Dryden coin by blending the words *witty* and *criticism*?

11. **SLANG** In the 14th century, Geoffrey Chaucer used the word *bones* as a name for what playing pieces used in games?

12. **EPONYMS** Did the word *Frisbee* come into English out of the hair-frizzing flying saucer stories of the 1950s, the early tall tales about a Yankee pitcher's bee-freezing fast ball, or from a game played by pie-eating, plate-throwing Yale students?

Level V (five points each)

13. **BRITICISMS** In Britain, is *a person who complains or whines all the time* called a wino, whinny, or whinger?

14. **HISTORY** What military vehicle is used only on land yet has parts with nautical names like *turret, hatch, hull*, and *deck* for no more logical reason than the fact that it was developed by the British navy?

15. **GENERAL QUESTIONS** Which country has more people who speak English: Australia, Canada, Britain, or the United States?

Level VI (six points each)

16. BORROWED WORDS What word that was borrowed from Russian in 1957 has the literal meaning of *traveling companion*?

17. EPONYMS Is Buckminster Fuller's eponym, *buckyball*, a type of molecule, table tennis, or dance?

18. WORD EVOLUTIONS In what order did the words *congressperson*, *congressman*, and *congresswoman* appear in English?

DID YOU KNOW ...

France's *Académie Française* was established in 1637 for the purpose of securing and maintaining standard French as pure as possible. It has survived in form until modern times and is as active and aggressive now as ever. In general, it defines *purity* as the absence of foreign words. Were purists of English ever to succeed in establishing a similar organization with the same philosophy and goal, the history of the language says it would be ignored by all but comedians.

BETHUMP'D LITE
GAME 20

Level I (one point each)

1. **AMERICANISMS** What *slang term for dollar* came from the frontier practice of using the hides of deer as a unit of trade with Indians?

2. **HOMOPHONES** What homophones are defined as *a mountain's highest point* and *to take a quick look?*

3. **WORD EVOLUTIONS** What do Philadelphians call the drink that is called *pop* in Chicago and *tonic* in Boston?

Level II (two points each)

4. **NAMES / NICKNAMES** What state's name came from that of the state from which it separated during the Civil War?

5. **BORROWED WORDS** What sneakers have a brand name that means *male roe deer* in South African Dutch?

6. **EUPHEMISMS** Is the *dickens*, as in "She scared the *dickens* out of him," an old time euphemism for dead chickens, Charles Dickens, or the devil?

Level III (three points each)

7. **WORD EVOLUTIONS** In 1909, what word came into com-

mon use from the word *omnibus?*

8. **TRUE OR FALSE** The word *salary* came from the Latin word *salarius*, which means *of salt.*

9. **WORD EVOLUTIONS** What word is defined as *an errand boy* in Scotland and as *a golfer's assistant* in the United States?

Level IV (four points each)

10. **TRUE OR FALSE** Language experts say, since those with small vocabularies have less cluttered minds, they are better able to think and solve problems.

11. **AUSTRALIANISMS** In Australia, is a *billabong* a kangaroo, a game like Ping-Pong, or a watering hole?

12. **ACRONYMS** In 1983, what acronym was coined for those known as *young urban professionals?*

Level V (five points each)

13. **NAMES / NICKNAMES** What high-speed bird is known as a *chaparral cock* in Texas and *snake eater* in New Mexico?

14. **WORD ORIGINS** What word came from the Greek word that is spelled *g-y-m-n-á-z-e-i-n* and means *to train or exercise naked?*

15. **BORROWED WORDS** Is the original Italian meaning of *confetti* little confessions, sweetmeats, or grated cheeses?

Level VI (six points each)

16. **GENERAL QUESTIONS** Which language is spoken by the largest number of people: English, French, German, or

Spanish?

17. LINGUISTICS What is held in common by *Esperanto* and *Interlingua*?

18. AUSTRALIANISMS In Australia, what happens when someone says, *"Shout them a drink"*: on signal, water bombs thrown; sheep are guided to a watering hole by shouting; or, someone buys a round of drinks?

Opinions about what constitutes 'proper' usage vary as much among professional word nerds as they do among non-professionals. Many professionals believe that what is right and what is wrong is a simple matter of preference or, at most, a question that is answered by how the majority actually use the language. In contrast, others prefer that *everyone* be taught to respect and abide by rules they consider important. This periodically leads to one camp sending shots across the bow of the other.

"Fussing about split infinitives is one of the more tiresome pastimes invented by nineteenth century grammarians."

Barbara Strang, Linguist
Modern English Structure,1962

BETHUMP'D LITE
GAME 21

Level I (one point each)

1. **TRUE OR FALSE** *Japlish* is a language that is a hybrid of Japanese and Polish.

2. **HOMOPHONES** A well-drilling adult male pig is a ___ who likes to ___ holes.

3. **HOLORIMIC PHRASES** What different phrase might be heard when someone shouts *"Ice cream"*?

Level II (two points each)

4. **SLANG** What single slang term is used to mean *teeth, helicopters, high-bouncing baseballs, machine guns,* and, as well, *motorcycles*?

5. **LETTER WORDS** By what letter word is the explosive *trinitrotoluene* more commonly known?

6. **PORTMANTEAU WORDS** In 1955, what word was coined by blending the words *motor* and *pedal*?

Level III (three points each)

7. **SLANG** What rhyming slang term appeared in English in 1964 defined as *notably relaxed* and was derived by analogy

from the observed fluid consistency of the manure of geese?

8. **WORD ORIGINS** Were *pussyfoot*, *road hog*, and *sneak thief* coined in Australia, Britain, Canada, or the United States?

9. **AMERICANISMS** What event in American history gave English the idioms *hit pay dirt*, *it's a goldmine*, *strike it rich*, and *to pan out*?

Level IV (four points each)

10. **BORROWED WORDS** What words did French borrow from English and spell *c-o-n-t-r-e-d-a-n-s-e*?

11. **TRUE OR FALSE** The idiom *worth one's salt* came from the time when Roman soldiers were paid with salt.

12. **CANADIANISMS** In the Province of Quebec, is *the government agency assigned to enforcing the use of French* facetiously known as the Babble Blasters, Lingo Lions, or Tongue Troopers?

Level V (five points each)

13. **WORD EVOLUTIONS** What other game's jargon provided baseball with a term to use when a home run is hit when the bases are loaded?

14. **NAMES / NICKNAMES** Because Henry Kaiser built ships amazingly fast during WWII, was he nicknamed Hammerdown Hank, Rub-a-dub-dub, or Sir Launchalot?

15. **HISTORY** Who coined the word *constitutionality*: Ben Franklin, Abe Lincoln, or Teddy Roosevelt?

Level VI (six points each)

16. NAMES / NICKNAMES What U.S. vice president called members of the media *nattering nabobs of negativism*?

17. BORROWED WORDS Was the original meaning of *Iowa*, which came from a Dakota Indian word, Get out of my way, I'm in the way, or The sleepy ones?

18. CALQUES What English idiom was borrowed directly into Dutch where it is expressed *je nek uitsteken*?

Some anthropologists believe Neanderthals, who lived from about 230,000 years ago to about 30,000 years ago, were incapable of clear articulation due to evidence that suggests their larynxes were high in their throats and their tongues were large and, thus, not very mobile.

In contrast, they say modern humans, who appeared over 100,000 years ago, must have had the ability to communicate and develop languages in modern form no later than about 40,000 years ago. Their thesis is based on bone finds and the oldest evidence of art, toolmaking, and other complex behaviors.

BETHUMP'D LITE
GAME 22

Level I (one point each)

1. **PORTMANTEAU WORDS** In 1896, what word was coined by blending the words *breakfast* and *lunch*?

2. **BORROWED WORDS** In 1690, what word evolved from the Malay word for *pickled fish sauce*, which sounded like it should be spelled *k-e-c-h-a-p*?

3. **EPONYMS** What ocean's name came from that of the Greek god *Atlas*?

Level II (two points each)

4. **HOMOPHONES** At the monastery, the old monk in charge of tending the chickens made sure his fellow ___ had two___ for supper each week.

5. **HISTORY** In the late 1700s, was Benjamin Franklin fearful that Irish, Italian, Spanish, or German would become the dominant language of Pennsylvania?

6. **HISTORY** Was the use of English first established in the New World in 1492, 1607, or 1776?

Level III (three points each)

7. **HOMOGRAPHS** The research center's accountants insisted that the scientist ___ the cost of her ___.

8. **BRITICISMS** In Britain, is a *sledge* a jack hammer, mall, or sled?

9. **BORROWED WORDS** In 1676, what word came into English from the Hindi word *bangla*, which means *house in the Bengal style*?

Level IV (four points each)

10. **HOMOGRAPHS** What homographs are defined as *having no validity* and *a sickly or disabled person*?

11. **WORD ORIGINS** Why is *Lucifer* a contradictory name for someone who is also known as *the Prince of Darkness*?

12. **HISTORY** What U.S. president was discovered to have what some called *"the vocabulary of a gangster"*?

Level V (five points each)

13. **TRUE OR FALSE** Unlike words written in English, Chinese ideographs convey meanings but not sounds.

14. **WORD EVOLUTIONS** In Samuel Johnson's dictionary of 1755, are *v*-words, *w*-words, or *x*-words listed among the *u*-words?

15. **WORD EVOLUTIONS** What are the meanings of the Frisian words that are spelled *k-o*, *l-a-m*, *b-o-a-t*, and *r-e-i-n*?

16. WORD ORIGINS What name that is formally used by mathematicians for the number 1 x 10^{100} was coined in 1938 by nine-year-old Milton Sirotta: one sirottion, one gadzillion, or a googol?

17. HOMOGRAPHS What homographs are defined as *an arithmetic unit* and *more devoid of emotion or feeling*?

18. CALQUES What English word was translated by French into *lune de miel*?

DID YOU KNOW ...

"Aristocratic and democratic tendencies in a nation often show themselves in its speech... It is often said, on the Continent at least, that the typical Englishman's self-assertion is shown by the fact that his is the only language in which the pronoun of the first person singular is written with a capital letter, while in some other languages it is the second person that is honoured by this distinction... ."

Otto Jespersen
Growth and Structure of the English Language, 1905

BETHUMP'D LITE
GAME 23

Level I (one point each)

1. **SLANG** *Yep* appeared in English in 1891, *yeah* in 1902, and both are used in place of what formal word?

2. **TRUE OR FALSE** *Grunts* is a name used for a species of fish whose grunting can sometimes be heard through the hulls of fishing boats.

3. **HOLORIMIC PHRASES** What other phrase might be heard when a hairy hippy jams a fist in the air and yells, *"Support Whirled Peas"*?

Level II (two points each)

4. **PORTMANTEAU WORDS** What word did the British coin by blending the words *channel* and *tunnel*?

5. **WORD EVOLUTIONS** What word once meant *a fire of bones*?

6. **WORD ORIGINS** What military rank's name came from the Latin word *privare*, which means *to deprive*?

Level III (three points each)

7. **TRUE OR FALSE** English arrived in Canada long before

French.

8. **CANADIANISMS** In Canada, is a *chesterfield* a large chest, a field on the east coast, or a sofa?

9. **TRUE OR FALSE** Most words that start with the letter *v* came from other languages.

Level IV (four points each)

10. **BORROWED WORDS** Are most of the words English borrows from other languages nouns, verbs, or adjectives?

11. **GENERAL QUESTIONS** What is held in common by the words *bomb*, *comb*, *dumb*, and *plumb*?

12. **BRITICISMS** In Britain, is a *toffee-nosed* kid a candy lover, a snob, or nosey?

Level V (five points each)

13. **PHONETICS** What is held in common by the *f* in *fast*, the *g-h* in *tough*, and the *p-h* in *phone*?

14. **BORROWED WORDS** What term did Dutch borrow from English and convert to a word spelled *d-i-e-p-v-r-i-e-s*?

15. **WORD EVOLUTIONS** What word that was spelled *s-e-e-l-y* and defined as *happy and blessed* in the 13th century is now defined as *foolish or lacking common sense*?

Level VI (six points each)

16. **HISTORY** In 1536, William Tyndale was strangled and burned at the stake because he translated what book into English?

17. NAMES / NICKNAMES What is particularly peculiar about the use of *Kiwi* in the corporate name *Kiwi International Air Lines*?

18. BORROWED WORDS In 1832, what word came into English from the Dutch word that is spelled *s-n-o-e-p-e-n* and means *to buy or eat on the sly*?

The King James version of the Bible, published in 1611, had a profound impact on the subsequent development of the English language. This is due, in part, to the fact that for vast numbers of people through many generations it was the book read most frequently or even, for some, the *only* book read. Its influence is evident in styles of speech and writing as well as in the general idiom of the language. Expressions from the Bible that for the most part were new to English in the 17th century are with us still—*an eye for an eye* (Exod. 21), *the skin of my teeth* (Job 19), *money is the root of all evil* (1 Tim. 6), *in the twinkling of an eye* (1 Cor. 15), and more.

BETHUMP'D LITE
GAME 24

Level I (one point each)

1. **NAMES / NICKNAMES** What is held in common by *flat-foot, smokey, fuzz,* and *bear*?

2. **BORROWED WORDS** What state's name came from an Aleut word that means *land that is not an island* and, originally, was phonetically spelled *a-l-a-k-s-h-a-k*?

3. **HOMOPHONES** The pecunious buyer bartered with the ___ as they walked down the steps to inspect the wine ___.

Level II (two points each)

4. **TRUE OR FALSE** *Catch* came from French while *caught* came from Old English.

5. **WORD ORIGINS** What animal's name came from the Latin words *porcus*, which means *pig*, and *spina*, which means *prickle*?

6. **BORROWED WORDS** In 1668, what word came into English from the Dutch word that means *rough drawing* and is spelled *s-c-h-e-t-s*?

Level III (three points each)

7. WORD ORIGINS What word evolved from the Latin word *avunculus*, which means *mother's brother*?

8. TRUE OR FALSE Since members of Canada's *Parti Quebecois* strive to maintain the purity of French by making illegal the use of words from other languages, the name *Quebec*, the root of *Quebecois*, originated in French.

9. HOMOPHONES A weird and crazy oriental market is a ___ ___.

Level IV (four points each)

10. WORD EVOLUTIONS What 20th century industry gave new definitions to the words *hardware, mouse*, and *chip*?

11. CANADIANISMS In Canada, is a *serviette* a female cadet, maid, or napkin?

12. TRUE OR FALSE In 1638, the word *coolie* came from a Chinese word and was at first spelled *k-u-l-i*.

Level V (five points each)

13. BRITICISMS Do the British call *the products sold by hardware stores* toolies, stiff stuff, or fixings?

14. ACCENTS In Liverpool, England, do those with a *Scouse* accent, such as the Beatles, say the plural of *you* as youse, yers, or y'all?

15. BORROWED WORDS What words did French borrow from English and spell *b-o-u-l-i-n-g-r-i-n*?

Level VI (six points each)

16. AMERICANISMS What word that is used around the world do linguists call *"The most successful Americanism ever"*?

17. CALQUES What Americanism was borrowed into French where it is translated *libre-service*?

18. EUPHEMISMS In the late 1990s, American entrepreneurs rushed to supply Japan's fashion industry when a huge unexpected demand developed for what *used* items that were sold to the Japanese under the euphemistic title *Vintage* ___?

DID YOU KNOW ...

In 1919, H.L. Mencken proclaimed the day will come when the divergence of American English from British English will result in mutually unintelligible languages, much in the way that French, Italian, and Spanish are distinguished from each other and their common ancestor Latin. By 1936, however, he tempered his position and believed that future scholars will view British English as a *dialect* of American English.

BETHUMP'D LITE

ANSWERS

BETHUMP'D LITE
ANSWERS

Bethump'd Lite—Game 1

1. fire / fire
2. cat
3. New York City
4. supercalifragilisticexpiali-docious
5. ate /eight
6. as soon as possible
7. motorcade
8. Mississippi
9. dis or diss
10. Catskills, from Dutch *Kats* and *Kill*
11. bass / bass
12. bayonet
13. rotten pot
14. graham cracker
15. the
16. 1 in 8
17. boob tube
18. peanut

Bethump'd Lite—Game 2

1. bark / bark
2. c—those who act first succeed
3. Johnny Appleseed (1774-1845)
4. guerilla / gorilla
5. motel
6. North & South *America*
7. a paddle
8. Levi's, or blue denim jeans
9. bolder / boulder
10. dandelion, from the French *dent de lion*
11. b—a left-handed person
12. junk food
13. False, it is French
14. car shocks
15. "A troop of boy scouts"
16. dollar
17. chortle, in *Through the Looking Glass*
18. 25

Bethump'd Lite—Game 3

1. Sunday / sundae
2. The cook had to bake a cake
3. Hawaii
4. read / read
5. pound / pound / pound / pound
6. Christopher Columbus
7. ukulele
8. way / whey / weigh
9. guy
10. electrocute
11. accountants
12. lynx / links
13. "It's going to rain."
14. wind / wind

15. funny money
16. *What you see is what you get*
17. post meridium
18. Eskimos

Bethump'd Lite—Game 4

1. squash / squash
2. smog
3. hamburger
4. the trees died
5. lives / lives
6. Delaware
7. petrol
8. foul / fowl
9. shabby
10. Supersonic Transport
11. tattoo
12. Brooklyn
13. "a well-oiled bicycle"
14. tick-tack-toe
15. cup of coffee
16. Scrooge, in *A Christmas Carol*
17. lunatic
18. it crashed

Bethump'd Lite—Game 5

1. an appetite for sweet foods
2. FBI
3. breakfast
4. border / boarder
5. saxophone, which appeared in 1851
6. raccoon

7. English
8. minute / minute
9. bat / bat
10. pears, that is, Bartlett pears
11. c—he escaped or ran away
12. chili / chilly / Chile
13. Manhattan
14. a diaper
15. soliloquy
16. superman
17. Geoffrey Chaucer, in the 14th century
18. nice

Bethump'd Lite—Game 6

1. boom box
2. couch potato
3. patience / patients
4. leaf
5. fair / fare
6. It's raining cats and dogs.
7. Tennessee
8. sunny-side up
9. situation + comedy
10. a wild dog
11. snorkel
12. accelerating
13. jockey
14. a boy
15. Montreal
16. time flies
17. Monday, Tuesday, Wednesday, Thursday, Friday, Saturday, and Sunday. *Tiu* and *Woden* were pagan gods. *Thor*

was Woden's son and *Frig* was his wife.
18. Flat Bush

Bethump'd Lite—Game 7

1. morning
2. hoarse / horse
3. can / can
4. Georgia
5. golf and cards
6. German
7. an elevator
8. lime / lime
9. Italian
10. a junkyard
11. boss
12. box / box
13. the Bronx
14. an apartment
15. English, less than 3% speak Irish
16. an arm and a leg
17. hippopotamus, from *hippos ho potámios*
18. The United Nations

Bethump'd Lite—Game 8

1. maid / made
2. the Morse code
3. crouton, from French *croûton*
4. c—they take more food than they can eat
5. Denver, Colorado
6. taught / taut

7. catalog
8. money
9. macadam
10. *Personal Computer*
11. Louisiana
12. a Cheshire cat's
13. rubber boots
14. boomerang
15. potato chips
16. garbage
17. amphibian, from Greek *amphibios*
18. 1973

Bethump'd Lite—Game 9

1. threw / through
2. *Prisoner Of War*
3. Big Ben
4. alphabet
5. macadamia
6. ski
7. chips
8. c—life is enjoyable
9. Ebonics, from *ebony* + *phonics*
10. soccer, as in "Soccer moms"
11. heel / heal
12. cotton candy
13. Gypsies, who really came from India
14. acrophobia
15. False, it was used in the same sense in the 16th century
16. Benjamin Franklin

17. French
18. a beer belly

Bethump'd Lite—Game 10

1. good-bye
2. feat / feet
3. close / close
4. dictionaries
5. *T*hank *G*od, *I*t's *F*riday
6. the United States'
7. Nevada
8. *C*entral *I*ntelligence *A*gency
9. a—she has excellent health
10. All-American
11. funnies
12. trunk
13. cereal
14. *N*ational *A*eronautics and *S*pace *A*dministration
15. gasohol
16. a foolish person
17. pitch / pitch / pitch / pitch
18. B.F. Goodrich coined it as a trademark.

Bethump'd Lite—Game 11

1. pretzel
2. "I love you"
3. sponge
4. stares / stairs
5. French's, from *r*épondez *s*'il *v*ous *p*laît (reply, if you please)
6. a low stool

7. present / present
8. cool
9. "How much is it?"
10. rap
11. jeans / genes
12. tycoon
13. bobby pins
14. False, at that time a shrew was a man
15. hooch
16. icicle
17. it's honest
18. don

Bethump'd Lite—Game 12

1. drive
2. bow / bow
3. argyle, a varicolored geometric design
4. pride / pride
5. the Reuben sandwich
6. "a crushing blow"
7. alligator
8. ham and eggs
9. sauna
10. a lousy pizza
11. barred / bard
12. a sweater
13. poltergeist
14. True, *girl* was variously spelled *gurle* and *girle* and was used to refer to both little boys and girls
15. a vacuum cleaner
16. turducken
17. letters of the alphabet

18. *E*xperimental *P*rototype *C*ommunity *O*f *T*omorrow

Bethump'd Lite—Game 13

1. "Howdy"
2. choose / chews
3. sideburns
4. *p-o-o-r* / *p-o-u-r* / *p-o-r-e*
5. *P*rofessional *G*olfers' *A*ssociation
6. two (birds) in the bush
7. flashlight
8. refuse / refuse
9. lover
10. August, from Latin *Augustus*
11. New York City, which ranked third below Berlin and Vienna
12. Animal House
13. each was coined as a trademark
14. bloody
15. quire / choir
16. damage control
17. 1,700-1,800
18. cyberspace, in *Burning Chrome*

Bethump'd Lite—Game 14

1. crow, as in *as the crow flies*
2. mood / mooed
3. zinnia
4. each is a slang term for *jail*
5. brayed / braid

6. supersonic
7. False, it means *squad leader* in *Japanese*
8. bonnet
9. pistol
10. dunce
11. Big Bertha
12. algebra
13. Wright: right / rite / write
14. bully
15. music, in *Outre-Mer* (1833-1834)
16. California
17. Mark Twain
18. Utopia, which in Greek means *no place*

Bethump'd Lite—Game 15

1. flea / flee
2. ESP
3. bawled / bald
4. "Girls love early birds."
5. tear / tear
6. overly emotional
7. France
8. Florida
9. mares eat oats
10. to quiet his car, a *silencer* is a muffler
11. cache / cash
12. twister to the slammer
13. *M*obile *A*rmy *S*urgical *H*ospital
14. Washington, in honor of George
15. sauerkraut

16. bacitracin
17. a person who says, "Not in my back yard" to the placement of landfills and other similar projects
18. 67

Bethump'd Lite—Game 16

1. twice baked cookies
2. mist / missed
3. bleachers
4. cymbals / symbols
5. coach
6. low stool
7. crazy
8. modem
9. tantalize
10. to hide something from Mom
11. Metro-Goldwyn-Mayer
12. catch-22
13. fat Tuesday
14. profit / prophet
15. airspeak
16. hot dog
17. Canada, which means village in Iroquoian
18. b—they are language-cluttering monstrosities

Bethump'd Lite—Game 17

1. groan / grown
2. July
3. True
4. sofa

5. True
6. r-o-d-e / r-o-a-d / r-o-w-e-d
7. starting a relationship
8. volcano
9. does / doze
10. flashy
11. Dan Rather
12. bayou
13. hard work
14. zero, it's an ideographic language and, thus, does not have an alphabet
15. first floor
16. ciao, which is a homophone of chow
17. mow / mow
18. bankrupt

Bethump'd Lite—Game 18

1. batter / batter
2. basketball
3. cheep / cheap
4. Braille
5. steaks / stakes
6. New Year's Eve
7. False, it was used as the short form of carriage as early as the 14th century
8. cities' names
9. bagman
10. a thumbtack
11. bottom of the bag
12. impudent
13. torpedo
14. 1929
15. False, he could not speak

English
16. the typewriter
17. flea market
18. trademark, for a cleaning solvent

Bethump'd Lite—Game 19

1. to a meeting of the *town council*
2. filly / Philly
3. Santa Claus
4. cereal / serial
5. mogul, which was borrowed in 1959
6. "*They ought to* do it."
7. console / console
8. fired
9. *USA Today*
10. witticism
11. dice
12. Yale students, who got their plated pies from nearby *Frisbie's* bakery
13. whinger
14. the tank
15. United States, with about 250-million
16. sputnik, which traveled with the Earth
17. a molecule, of extremely stable carbon$_{60}$
18. congressman (1780), congresswoman (1917), congressperson (1972)

Bethump'd Lite—Game 20

1. buck, from *buckskin*
2. peak / peek
3. soda
4. West Virginia
5. Reebok®, from *ree* (roe) + *boc* (buck)
6. the devil
7. bus
8. True
9. caddy
10. False, they say the *larger* the vocabulary the better one can think and solve problems
11. a watering hole
12. yuppies, from *y-u-p* + *-pies*
13. roadrunner
14. gymnasium
15. sweetmeats
16. English, which is second only to Chinese
17. each is an artificial language.
18. someone buys a round of drinks

Bethump'd Lite—Game 21

1. False, it's a hybrid of *Jap*anese and Eng*lish*
2. boar / bore
3. "I scream"
4. choppers
5. TNT

6. moped
7. loosey-goosey
8. the United States
9. the California Gold Rush of 1849
10. country dance
11. True
12. Tongue Troopers
13. bridge, the card game
14. Sir Launchalot
15. Ben Franklin coined it in 1787
16. Spiro T. Agnew, vice president under Nixon
17. The sleepy ones
18. stick your neck out

Bethump'd Lite—Game 22

1. brunch
2. ketchup
3. Atlantic
4. friars / fryers
5. German
6. 1607, with the settlement of Jamestown
7. project / project
8. sled
9. bungalow
10. invalid / invalid
11. Lucifer, in Latin, means *bearer of light*
12. Richard Nixon
13. True
14. *v*-words, because *v* was used as the consonant form of *u*

15. cow, lamb, boat, rain
16. googol
17. number / number
18. honeymoon

Bethump'd Lite—Game 23

1. yes
2. True
3. Support World Peace
4. chunnel
5. bonfire, from *bon* (bone) + *fyre* (fire)
6. private
7. False, French was first by about a century
8. sofa
9. True
10. nouns
11. each has a silent *b*
12. snob
13. each represents the *same* sound
14. deep-freeze
15. silly
16. the Bible
17. Kiwi is not only a fruit, it's *a bird that can't fly*
18. snoop

Bethump'd Lite—Game 24

1. each is a slang term for *police officer*
2. Alaska's
3. seller / cellar
4. True

5. porcupine
6. sketch
7. uncle
8. False, it's from an Algonquin Indian word that means *narrow passage*
9. bizarre / bazaar
10. computer
11. napkin
12. False, it came from a Hindi word
13. fixings
14. youse
15. bowling green
16. okay, which appeared March 23, 1839
17. self-service
18. Sneakers, with the strongest demand for those made in the 1980s

SELECT BIBLIOGRAPHY

AYTO, JOHN (1990), *Dictionary of Word Origins* (Little, Brown and Company, New York)

BRYSON, BILL (1990), *The Mother Tongue* (William Morrow, New York)

COMRIE, BERNARD, STEPHEN MATTHEWS, and MARIA POLINSKY, Eds. (1996), *The Atlas of Languages* (Facts on File, New York)

CRYSTAL, DAVID (1995), *The Cambridge Encyclopedia of the English Language* (Cambridge University Press, Cambridge)

JESPERSEN, OTTO (1938), *Growth and Structure of the English Language*, 9th edition, (Doubleday, New York)

JOHNSON, SAMUEL (orig. 1755), *A Dictionary of the English Language* (Todd's edition., pub. 1994, Barnes & Noble Books, New York)

McARTHUR, TOM, Ed. (1992), T*he Oxford Companion to the English Language* (Oxford University Press, Oxford and New York)

McCRUM, ROBERT, WILLIAM CRAN, and ROBERT MacNeil (1993), *The Story of English*, revised ed., (Penguin Books, New York and London)

MENCKEN, H.L. (1936), *The American Language* (Alfred A. Knopf, New York)

MERRIAM-WEBSTER, *Merriam-Webster's Collegiate Dictionary*, 10th ed. (Springfield, MA)

ONIONS, C.T., Ed. (1966), *The Oxford Dictionary of English Etymology* (Oxford University Press, Oxford and New York)

PARTRIDGE, ERIC (1983), *Origins* (Greenwich House, New York)

STRANG, BARBARA M.H. (1991), *A History of English* (Routledge, London and New York)